German Fighter Ace Walter Nowotny

German Fighter Ace
Walter Nowotny
An Illustrated Biography

Werner Held

Schiffer Military History
Atglen, PA

Book translation by Christine Wisowaty

Book Design by Ian Robertson.

Library of Congress Control Number: 200692694

Printed in China.
ISBN: 0-7643-2527-2

This book was originally published in German under the title
Der Jagdflieger Walter Nowotny by Motorbuch Verlag

We are interested in hearing from authors with book ideas on related topics.

Published by Schiffer Publishing Ltd.
4880 Lower Valley Road
Atglen, PA 19310
Phone: (610) 593-1777
FAX: (610) 593-2002
E-mail: Info@schifferbooks.com.
Visit our web site at: www.schifferbooks.com
Please write for a free catalog.
This book may be purchased from the publisher.
Please include $3.95 postage.
Try your bookstore first.

In Europe, Schiffer books are distributed by:
Bushwood Books
6 Marksbury Avenue
Kew Gardens
Surrey TW9 4JF, England
Phone: 44 (0) 20 8392-8585
FAX: 44 (0) 20 8392-9876
E-mail: Info@bushwoodbooks.co.uk.
Visit our website at: www.bushwoodbooks.co.uk
Free postage in the UK. Europe: air mail at cost.
Try your bookstore first.

Contents

Foreword

Werner Held asked me, Walter Nowotny's former *Geschwaderkommodore*, to write the foreword to this book.

I gladly fulfill this request, because the author has succeeded in his illustrated book to give a vivid account of Nowotny the man, soldier, and fighter pilot, as if he were still with us. So, death does not only separate, but unites by ending the eternal cycle of the living.

Walter Nowotny belonged to the wiry and athletic young fighter pilots, who quickly surpassed their successful and experienced mentors in ability in the "Grünherzgeschwader." However, it was not only his aeronautical abilities, his marksmanship, and his superior air combat tactics that set him apart from the other successful pilots of *Jagdgeschwader* 54. It was more so discipline, courage, and austerity combined with a healthy ambition that led him to the top of the German *Jagdflieger-Asse*. His well known name, that was always associated with his achievements in the *Wehrmachtbericht*, resonated well not only amongst the *Landser* of the northern section of the Eastern Front, from Leningrad to Ilmensee, but also among the civilian population at home.

However, "Nowi's" ambition had boundaries. His ambition stopped at the safety of his *Rottenflieger* and his *Schwarm*. He felt close to his pilots and was happy about their achievements, which in turn created trust. Nowotny had an especially considerate and appreciative relationship with the men of his ground crew. They all knew that the "boss" understood that their reliable technical work was necessary for the success of the pilots. From this realization a sworn companionship formed between "Nowi," his pilots, and the men of his ground crew.

Filled with the intoxication of youth and a stark masculinity, Walter Nowotny alternated from military strictness to letting himself go, from disciplined flight and serious missions on the front to overflowing *Lebensfreude* (joy of life) after landing.

But his love was for his parents' house and his Austrian homeland. He was a religious man who lived by his beliefs, drew power from, and let himself be guided by them.

"Nowi" will always remain in our thoughts.

Formerly
Kommodore
Jagdgeschwader 54 "Grünherz"

Introduction

Peace and quiet overcomes a visitor when s/he stands in front of the memorial in Epe bei Bremsche, where Major Walter Nowotny found his death on November 8, 1944. Surrounded by fields, and embedded in the passing of the seasons lays a small piece of earth in the middle of rural surroundings. The land here is flat on the *Mittellandkanal*. It is only interrupted by groups of trees and shrubs. The vastness of the sky—frequently covered by drifting clouds—conveys a feeling of endlessness. Every now and then, the stillness is broken by a sports plane coming from Achmer Airport nearby, with a steady hum as it passes by. The wind drowns out the monotone buzzing of the highway.

The visitor, who is lost in thought, standing in front of the well-kept grounds, will automatically be taken back to a time in which fear, restlessness, and noisiness governed the day. The monotone buzzing gets closer, and in one's mind's eye storms of bombs in the east bring death and disaster. The steady humming of the sports plane turns into a dull howling, and a lone *Turbinenjäger* hunts as quick as lighting in the cloudy sky. The clattering sounds of a tractor driving by turn into a hammering of aircraft weapons and cannons.

The memorial in Epe, erected by Walter Nowotny's comrades, is the meeting place every year on his day of death for those who in hard times looked at him in reverence—also of the younger generation, who heard of his achievements.

He is not thought about only here. In November flowers, wreaths, and sprays decorate the grave of the fighter pilot in the *Zentralfriedhof* in Vienna. When ignorant visitors walk along the honored graves of Vienna, fresh flowers reveal the spot where Walter Nowotny found his last place of rest. He rests in the middle of graves of other Austrian dignitaries as the only soldier.

This illustrated book retraces the life of a young man, a life like many German fighter pilots led, until it abruptly ended at the height of glory—and nevertheless remains unforgotten in the consciousness and memory of many.

Former enemies speak in admiration of the achievements of the German soldier, and many former *Luftwaffenflugzeugführer* are received and celebrated with much respect in the western world. The countless number of friendships that are still today being formed—40 years after this disastrous war—bear witness.

Who was Walter Nowotny, and what achievements did this young fighter pilot accomplish? After 40 years he is still a brilliant role model and idol of a generation—how is that possible?

How did it come to it, that my interest in him was roused, and that as a result I can present my investigations in this book?

The preparatory work to my illustrated book about the mission of German *Tagjäger* in World War II brought me initially to the Nürnberg picture journalist Karl Schnörrer—called "Quax" by his flying companions—then to Walter Nowotny. The tears in Schnörrer's eyes, as I handed him a picture with a laughing Walter Nowotny, were the reason that I from then on occupied myself intensively with the life of this fighter pilot. Schnörrer was a *Rottenflieger* and friend of Nowotny. I then visited Nowotny's brother in Linz/Donau, drove to Vienna with him to his grave in the *Zentralfriedhof*, stood before his birthplace in Gmünd, and despite the rain, experienced the countryside of the woodlands—and soon Walter Nowotny was a stranger no more. Former flying companions provided pictures for me from personal albums, and my collection of documents became more and more extensive. The family Nowotny thereby supported me generously. A further trip to Austria was undertaken, and Mr. Schnörrer was repeatedly interviewed. In his last letter—unfortunately he died on September 24, 1979, from the long-term consequences of his war injuries—he spoke about my "book of the heart." Walter Nowotny became as familiar to me as my own brother.

This illustrated book shows the human as well as the aeronautical side of the development of Walter Nowotny: from the carefree early days to his sudden death on November 8, 1944. It was my goal to make Walter Nowotny, the man, known. He was close to his family, especially his mother, and loved his Austrian homeland. Here is the place to search for the reasons that gave him the power and the will for extraordinary achievements. Because of his winsome nature he made many friends, and he was always ready to give more than to receive. He knew that his ground crew was to be thanked for his victories, and he never failed to tell them that. They would go through thick and thin for their "Nowi."

Three years on the Eastern Front in the "Grünherzgeschwader" (JG 54), where Nowotny served until February 1944, brought him to the top of the German fighter pilots. He defeated 255 enemy planes in heavy air battle. He was unremittingly dedicated to his job, and cooperated well with his *Rottenflieger*, the so-called "Katschmareks," and his true men in the "black overalls," the ground crew. Rich experiences on the Front and specific skills for leadership qualified the then 23 year old *Hauptmann* to take over the management of *Schulgeschwader* 101 and *Jagdfliegerschule* I in Pau, in Southern France. The commander's nerves became understandably challenged and tense. Soon he did not feel well in this position. Nevertheless, many instances are known where he helped desperate young flyers in a fatherly manner with difficulties during their schooling.

In the summer of 1944, Nowotny—who in the meantime advanced to major—was presented with a new assignment that he received with excitement and enthusiasm: the formation and deployment of a Me 262-*Erprobungskommando* that carried his name. General Galland later said about Nowotny:

"He was the best young man that Germany had. He was an excellent fighter pilot, who brought with him a special talent for higher command. Even though he was only 24 years old, he was right for *Geschwaderkommodore*... I think he was in every respect an exceptionally good man."

The air combat over Germany had continually worsened. The tremendous efforts in the first half of 1944 did not bring about the success that was hoped for. Even though the air armament was going full blast, the number of fighter planes being produced—Me 109s and Fw 190s—increased, and the training of young pilots in the *Ausbildungsgeschwader* was carried out unrelentingly with all might, the number of allied *Jäger* and *Bomberverbände* grew stronger and stronger in comparison to the German fighter defense of the *Reichsverteidigung*. Germany's cities were bombed even further, and the arms factories were smashed to pieces. Leadership and propaganda fed the hopes of the German people for the awaited "Wunderwaffen."

In the meantime, experienced pilots in Lechfeld were retrained for a new type of plane, on which the *Luftwaffe* and many successful fighter pilots set their hopes. It was the first operational *Turbinenjäger* of the world: the Me 262. With their own planes of this type, a small group gained their first experiences in battle. Under *Hauptmann* Werner Thierfelder, a destroyer pilot of ZG 26, the first shots were successful. *Leutnant* Schreiber shot down the first "Mosquito," and *Feldwebel* Lennartz the first Bomber B-17 with a Me 262. On July 18, 1944, *Hauptmann* Thierfelder was involved in a fatal crash. *Hauptmann* Horst Geyer—until now *Erprobungskommando* 25—was put in charge of *Erprobungskommando* Me 262. Another small commando was set up under Günter Wegmann in Erfurt-Bindersleben. But before the work on the short runways and the aeronautical facilities was completed, an order came for the relocation to Achmer. Göring put Major Nowotny in charge of the deployment of a Me 262-*Jagdverband*.

From the *Erprobungskommando* Lechfeld Nowotny chose the best pilots, and transferred together with the "Kommando Wegmann" at the beginning of October 1944 with 30 planes to Achmer and Hesepe, north of Osnabrück. Both groups arrived at the same time in Achmer; Nowotny appointed Wegmann to be his *Adjutant*. *Oberleutnant* Bley assumed leadership of the *Staffel* in Achmer, and *Leutnant* Schall was entrusted with the *Staffel* in Hesepe.

Both places in the landing zone of the enemy *Bomber* and *Jagdverbände* had the necessary available runway length. A few days later "Kommando Nowotny" had the first losses due to the American "Mustang"-*Jäger*. Two planes were attacked at takeoff. Another Me 262 was the victim of a "Mustang" during landing.

Major Nowotny saw to it that the takeoff and landing of the Me 262 was secured by the *Platzschutzstaffel*. Experienced pilots built an air shield during the dangerous takeoff and landing phases of the Me 262 "Turbos."

The commando flew missions and was successful. But these successes were also accompanied by painful losses. Multiple accidents took place. Swarms of birds or operating errors of the inexperienced pilots were mostly the cause. Nowotny became more and more uneasy and irritated. He himself could defeat two further opponents.

On November 7, 1944, General Galland came with *Generaloberst* Keller to Achmer to inspect the facilities. While making rounds, the position of the airports was said to be a problem. *Generaloberst* Keller, who was at this time responsible for the aeronautical recruits, touched on the question of the pilots' love of combat. This topic was aimed in the direction of Göring's accusations concerning the "cowardly" pilots. The mood was therefore not the best.

The next morning—it was 8 November—strong allied *Bomberverbände* with *Jagdbegleitschutz* were reported. The generals wanted to observe the missions of the *Kommando* and postponed their departure. The *Rotten* Wegmann and Schall received a combat order. Both *Rotten* shot down a "Mustang." Then *Leutnant* Schall reported the shooting of his *Rottenflieger*, and shortly thereafter: "My plane is on fire, bale out!"

Now nothing was holding back Nowotny, and he called after his driver. "I'm starting." Galland's cries, "Stay here, Nowotny!" remained unheard. A pilot in Hesepe received the command to meet Nowotny in the air after takeoff. Major Nowotny had to fly this mission alone because a *Rottenflieger* cancelled his takeoff due to a turbine that caught fire.

Nowotny flew into the hostile formation, and reported shortly thereafter the firing of a Bomber. Over the radio a nervous call was heard: "Shit, shit, my engine!" The following words could not be understood. In the distance a Me 262 with a burning turbine was seen diving out of the clouds, and its angle of inclination became steeper and steeper. The "Turbo" disappeared behind the horizon. Shortly thereafter a strong detonation. Everyone who saw it did not want to believe that it was Nowotny's plane.

But there was no doubt: Major Nowotny was dead. The exact cause will never be established. American fighter pilots did not report a shooting down of a Me 262 during this time, even though two "Mustangs" were pursuing a crashing Me 262, and then flew over *Platz Achmer* in a low-level flight. Was Major Nowotny shot down by his own anti-aircraft artillery? An eyewitness in Epe saw the burning "Turbo" explode in the air before it hit the ground. The parachute hung half open under a tree, so it was assumed that Nowotny tried to bale out. A flyer's life ended after the shooting of the 258th air opponent.

In the German edition of his book *Die grofle Arena* (*The Big Arena*), Piere Clostermann, the great French fighter pilot, writes:

"Walter Nowotny has fallen... This evening his name is often mentioned in the mess halls. With respect, almost affection, everyone is speaking of memories that connect themselves with him. It is the first time that I hear this tone in the RAF; for the first time I am also observing how a peculiar solidarity beyond single tragedies and prejudices between all fighter pilots is openly expressed...

...Today we greet a brave enemy with whom fate caught up, declare Nowotny as one of our own, who took part in this world in which neither ideologies nor hate, nor boundaries counted. Comradeship has nothing to do with patriotism, democracy, national socialism, or notion of mankind. Today everyone senses that instinctively. Those who shrug their shoulders cannot understand—they are not fighter pilots... What a shame, that this man did not wear our uniform. He would have been a great guy."

The pictures of this book can better describe the life of Walter Nowotny than words. Born and raised in the protective care of his family, he was influenced from a time that spoke especially to youth. Mentally agile, with a great understanding of technical matters, he was drawn to flying. During his fighter pilot training he was one of the best pupils of the well-known Austrian World War flyer and stunt pilot, *Hauptmann* Julius Arigi. The first independent fighter missions over the Baltic Sea demonstrated the amazing talent of this young flyer. Slowly and continually he climbed the ladder of success, until he stood as the top of all German fighter pilots after three years of deployment on the Eastern Front.

His extraordinary talents in leadership characterized his last year of life. Promoted to Major at only 24 years old, Walter Nowotny is a role model for many—then as well as today.

Childhood and School Days

The woodlands—lower Austrian border area—Walter Nowotny's homeland. The desolate, wooded low mountain range, along with its inhabitants, influenced Walter Nowotny.

Walter Nowotny is born in this house in Gmünd on December 7, 1920.

The three "Nowotny boys" (1924): Rudolf, the oldest, Hubert, and Walter (left).

The *Franz-Josefs-Bahn* train station in Schwarzenau, where the *Bchnbeamte* Rudolf Nowotny lived with his family from 1925 until 1925.

Walter as a school beginner (front left) in the *Volksschule* Schwarzenau (1927).

Enjoying vacation with a brother of his mother in Höritz, in Böhmerwald (1931).

An idyllically situated forest lake is often a destination for an excursion and swimming for the "Nowotny boys" and their friends during the summer months.

Walter (second from the left) with friends during an excursion in the lower Austrian *Weinsberg-Gebiet*.

Right: Group picture taken during a long hike in the woodlands.

1935 - The soccer team of the *Bundesoberrealschule* Waidhofen/Thai that Nowotny attends. After his father's transfer to Mistelbach, north of Vienna, he transfers to the *Oberschule* in Laa/Thaya. Nowotny to the right in the middle row, kneeling.

The 10 year old Walter as a choirboy in the Zwettl convent (1930).

Nowotnys' Family picture, Christmas 1936.

The *Oberschüler* Walter Nowotny.

In the summer of 1936 Nowotny secretly visits the Olympic games in Berlin. Since this time his athletic ambition shows no more boundaries. In 1937 he takes first place in the javelin throw.

1938 - the victorious *HJ-Staffel* from Mistelbach. Walter (middle) with his successful sports comrades.

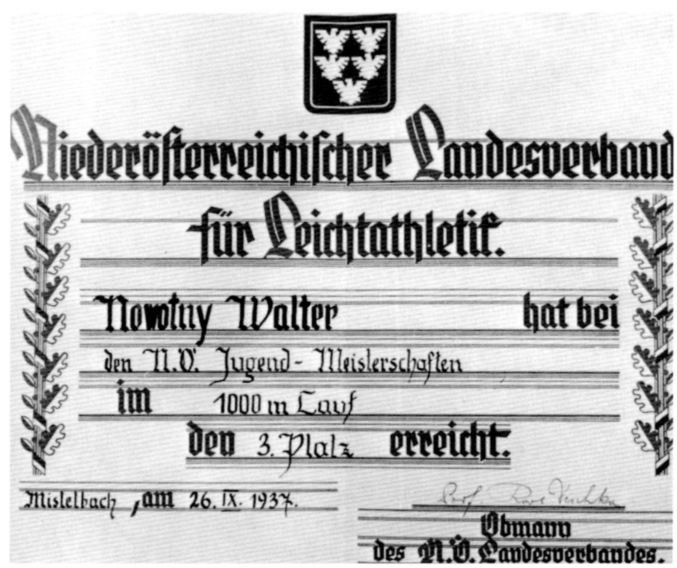

Niederösterreichischer Landesverband
für Leichtathletik.
Nowotny Walter hat bei
den N.Ö. Jugend-Meisterschaften
im 1000 m Lauf
den 3. Platz erreicht.
Mistelbach, am 26. IX. 1937.
Obmann
des N.Ö. Landesverbandes.

According to the certificate of the *N. Ö. Landesverbandes für Leichtalthletik* (N. Ö. National Association for Track-and-Field Sports), Nowotny reaches third place in the 1000-meter run.

Aviation Training

In May 1938 Walter Nowotny successfully completes his school-leaving exam at the *Oberschule* in Laa. A half year of hard work in the *Reichsarbeitsdienst* (RAD) follows. Nowotny voluntarily does his military basic training from 1 October until 15 November 1939 in the *2. Flieger-Ausbildungsregiment 62* in Quedlinburg.

The *Fliegersoldat* Nowotny in the student company of the *Luftkriegschule* 5, Breslau-Schöngarten (November 16, 1939-June 30, 1940)

Christmas 1939. First vacation in Mistelbach with his brother Rudolf.

Left: Finally: First flight with the flying instructor in the Heinkel He 72 "Kadett." A special experience for the young flyers. Right: Soon his first solo flight. The flight instructor winks encouragingly at his protégé.

A long-distance flight with an Arado Ar 68.

In the meantime, Walter Nowotny is transferred to *Jagdfliegerschule 5* in Wien-Schwechat. He actually wants to be a *Stuka-Flieger*, but his "personal guide" decides differently. Under the wing of *Hauptmann* Julius Arigi he learns the ABCs of being a fighter pilot, and is considered one of the best in the course.

Aerial photograph taken during a long-distance flight to Regensburg. Under the left wing, the Danube with Walhalla.

Karl Schnörrer also finds himself in Wien-Schwechat for fighter training since May 1940. In the course of the following years a true friendship between "Nowi" and "Quax" develops that will outlast Walter's early death.

The good, old Junkers W34 and Focke-Wulf 58 "Weihe" are used for blind flying schooling and for long-distance flights. In the picture below (far right), Schnörrer with course comrades in front of the Fw 58 "Weihe" planes.

The preferred "Vogel" of the flight schools is the Arado Ar 96. Its beautiful form, as well as its good flying characteristics, are probably the reason for this.

On March 1, 1940, Nowotny is promoted to *Fahnenjunker-Gefreiten*, and shortly thereafter (April 1, 1940) to *Fahnenjunker-Unteroffizier*. On July 1, 1940, the newly promoted *Fähnrich* is happy about his new rank.

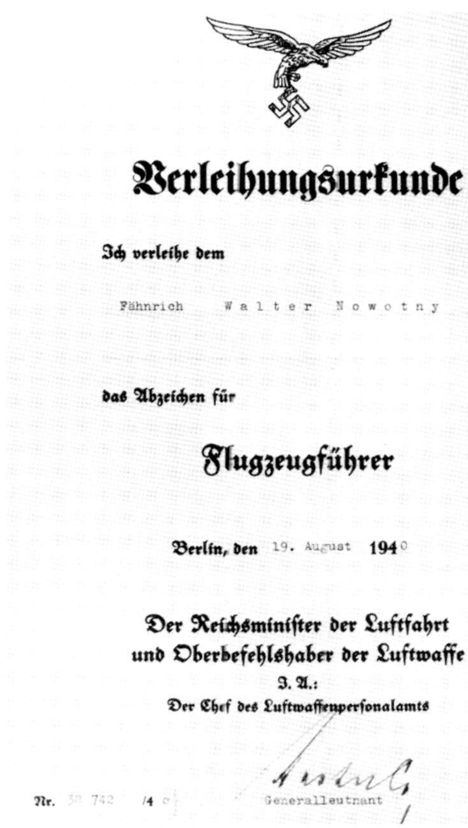

Verleihungsurkunde

Ich verleihe dem

Fähnrich Walter Nowotny

das Abzeichen für

Flugzeugführer

Berlin, den 19. August 1940

Der Reichsminister der Luftfahrt
und Oberbefehlshaber der Luftwaffe
I. A.:
Der Chef des Luftwaffenpersonalamts

Nr.

Generalleutnant

The Pilot's insignia for *Fähnrich* Nowotny on August 19, 1940.

Three proud *Fähnriche* of the *Jagdfliegerschule* Wien-Schwechat: (from the left) Walter Nowotny, Paul Galland (the youngest brother of Adolf Galland), and Ulrich Burkhardt.

September 1940—on leave. Nowotny with his father in the garden in Mistelbach.

Nowotny receives his actual fighter pilot training (retraining on the Bf 109) from 1 August until November 15, 1940, in Wien-Schwechat. The well-known dangers of the Bf 109—pulling of the plane at takeoff—give flight instructors many gray hairs.

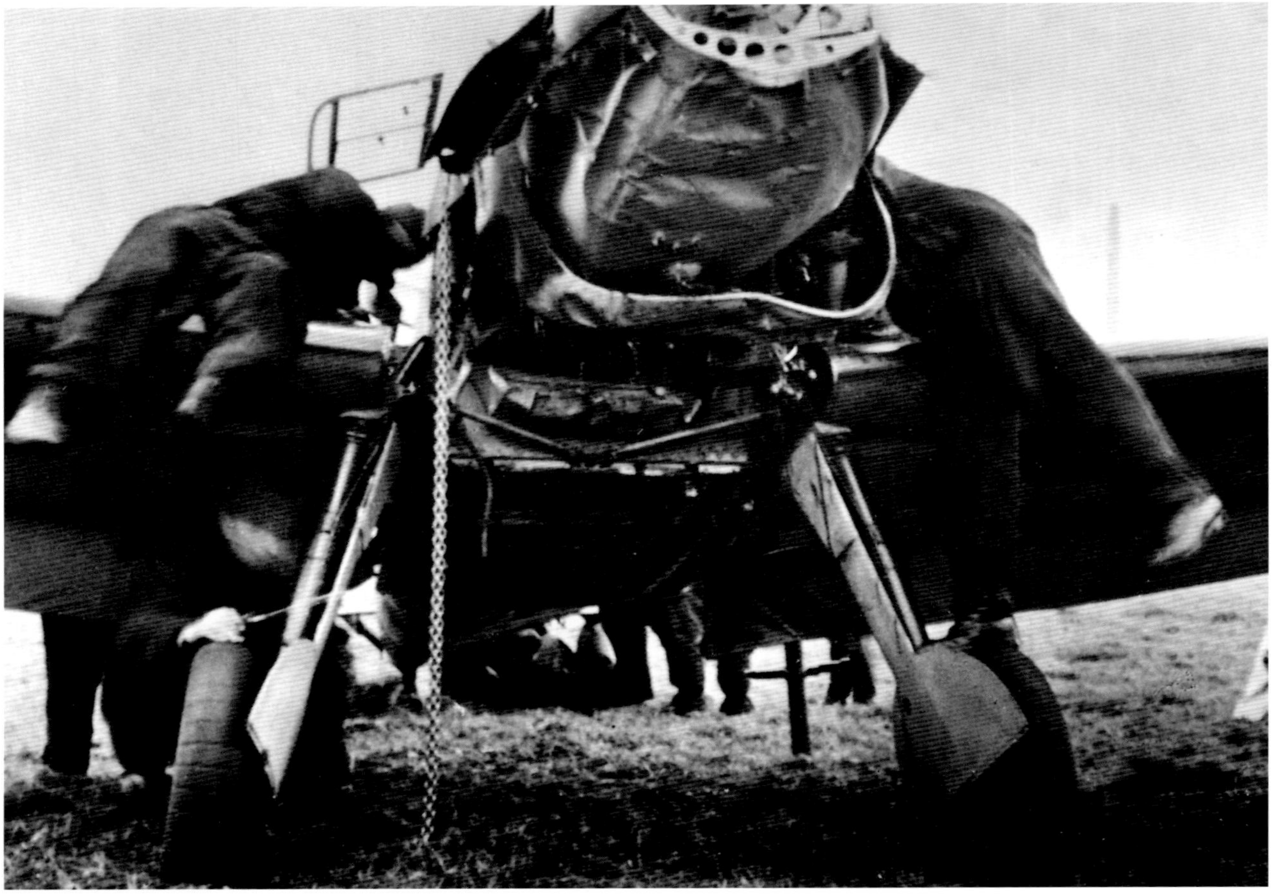

The young *Fähnrich* is not spared the difficulties with the "109." Once during landing he forgets to lower the undercarriage and performs a belly landing. The ground crew must expend all its energy to make the plane ready for takeoff again. Nowotny's admiration for their achievements starts here.

Missions on the Eastern Front

Reichsmarschall Göring's visit to the *Jagdfliegerschule* Wien-Schwechat brings Walter Nowotny a pleasant change. He is transferred with two other comrades to *I. Ergänzungs-Jagdgruppe* Merseburg on November 16, 1940. With this premature transfer the three young pilots receive recognition for their achievements. The fighter group has the assignment to protect the *Leuna-Werke* and its barrage balloons from the air. The expectations that the three pilots have in this new assignment are not fulfilled: the air enemies stay out!

In December 1940 Nowotny is transferred to *Ergänzungs-Staffel* JG 54, and is assigned to a Front unit for the first time. Here he sets his own boundaries. From 23 February until March 25, 1941, *Fähnrich* Nowotny is with 9. JG 54—the so-called "Teufelstaffel." Experienced pilots take him under their wings. He puts the finishing touches to ground missions and escort assignments for German ship units across the Baltic Sea. For the first time he experiences how ferruginous the air can become for a fighter pilot.

From March 25, 1941, to March 10, 1942, Nowotny flies in the *Stabstaffel* of *Ergänzungs-Jagdgruppe* JG 54. The young fighter pilot scouts out his opponents in the air and attacks them independently. Originally scheduled to be promoted on April 1, 1941, Walter Nowotny is promoted to *Leutnant* on 1 February, and is now an *Offizier*.

Oberleutnant Eggers, *Staffel-Kapitän* of *Ergänzungs-Jagdgruppe* JG 54.

The former Russian airports, that are now used by the German *Luftwaffe*, all show the same: planes of all types, destroyed or unusable. The element of surprise is completely successful here.

Leutnant Henkemeier—the "blonde Urgermane," as he is jokingly called—brings home both of his first air victories. *Leutnant* Nowotny congratulates the successful comrade after the landing of his plane.

The return of each comrade is cheerfully greeted—with youthful high-spirits. From the left: *Lt.* Kretschmer, *Lt.* Henkemeier, *Lt.* Nowotny with a swim vest, a technical officer, and the *Staffelkapitän*, *Oltn.* Eggers.

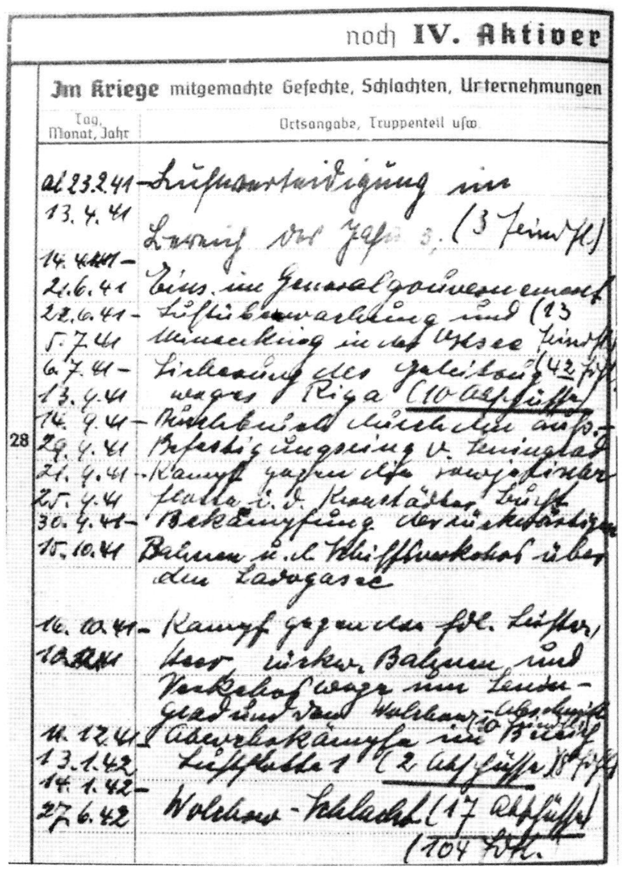

noch IV. Aktiver

Im Kriege mitgemachte Gefechte, Schlachten, Unternehmungen

Tag, Monat, Jahr	Ortsangabe, Truppenteil usw.
ab 23.2.41– 13.4.41	Luftverteidigung im Bereich der ... (3 Feindfl.)
14.4.41– 21.6.41	Eins. im Generalgouvernement
22.6.41– 5.7.41	Luftüberwachung und (13 ...) ... in der Ostsee
6.7.41– 13.9.41	... Riga (10 Abschüsse)
14.9.41–	[illegible]
29.9.41	[illegible]
21.9.41– 25.9.41	Kampf gegen ...
30.9.41– 15.10.41	Bekämpfung ... den Ladogasee
16.10.41–	Kampf gegen ...
11.12.41	[illegible]
13.1.42	Luftflotte 1 (2 Abschüsse ...)
14.1.42– 27.6.42	Wolchow-Schlacht (17 Abschüsse) (104 ...)

28

Entries in *Lt.* Nowotny's service record book. The assignments that are given to the fighter pilots are varied.

On July 19, 1941, *Lt.* Nowotny shoots down two Russian I 153s over the island Ösel during a free hunt. The fuse gauge indicates that it is time for the return flight. A plane with a white "snout" flies behind the successful Bf 109. But the supposed "Katschmarek" is a Russian, whose weapons hit the German planes hard. Nowotny circles out the enemy and shoots him down, but then the engine stalls. The "109" glides down in the direction of the coast, touches down on water, and Nowotny paddles in an inflatable raft towards the coast. After three days he is completely exhausted as he washes ashore at Mikelbaka. A coastal artillery unit of the marines takes care of the pilot.

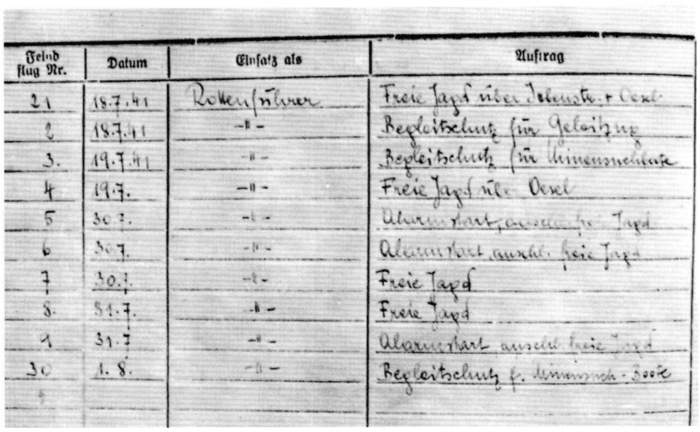

Feindflug Nr.	Datum	Einsatz als	Auftrag
21	18.7.41	Rottenführer	Freie Jagd über [illegible] + Oesel
2	18.7.41	-"-	Begleitschutz für Geleitzug
3.	19.7.41	-"-	Begleitschutz für Minensuchboote
4	19.7.	-"-	Freie Jagd über Oesel
5	30.7.	-"-	Alarmstart, anschl. fr. Jagd
6	30.7.	-"-	Alarmstart anschl. freie Jagd
7	30.7.	-"-	Freie Jagd
8.	31.7.	-"-	Freie Jagd
9	31.7.	-"-	Alarmstart anschl. freie Jagd
30	1.8.	-"-	Begleitschutz f. Minensuch-Boote

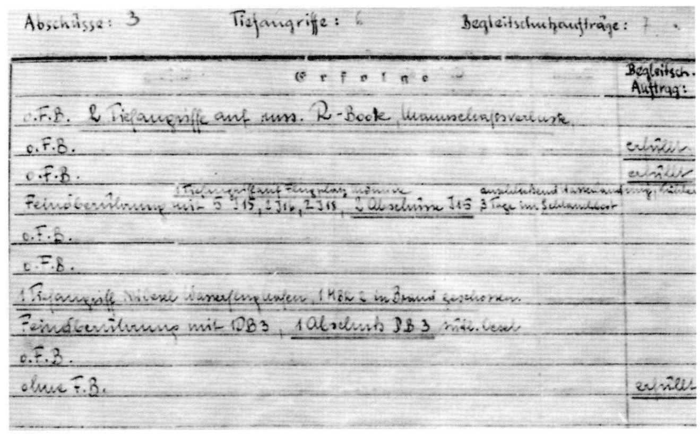

Abschüsse: 3 Tiefangriffe: 6 Begleitschutzaufträge: 7

Erfolge	Begleitsch. Auftrag:
o.F.B. 2 Tiefangriffe auf russ. R-Boote, [illegible]	
o.F.B.	erfüllt
o.F.B.	erfüllt
Feindberührung mit 5 I 15, 2 I 16, 2 I 18, 2 Abschüsse I 15 [illegible] 3 Tage im Schlauchboot	
o.F.B.	
o.F.B.	
1 Tiefangriff [illegible], 1 [illegible] in Brand geschossen.	
Feindberührung mit 1 DB 3, 1 Abschuß DB 3 [illegible] Oesel	
o.F.B.	
ohne F.B.	erfüllt

The experience under Mission No. 34 is entered in Nowotny's book of flight achievements. The third air victory is not confirmed because there is no witness. The picture below shows him during a later visit of the marine unit.

"Nowi"—as his comrades call him—has, since he was a child, a weakness for everything that has to do with engines So he passes all of the driving tests for all classes.

Lt. Nowotny and *Uffz.* "Toni" Döbele. Anton Döbele flies later in Nowotny's famous *Schwarm*.

Gefreite Schnörrer—with *Ergänzungs-Jagdgruppe* 54 in combat as well—talks shop with his friend Kolotzi and *Uffz.* Wulfers.

In August 1941 the drive to Königsberg is the young *Leutnant*'s undoing. His "109" has to stay in the hangar for a few days, which is a good opportunity for a short vacation. On a street that is wet from the rain he loses control of his vehicle and drives into the middle of the forest. He lands himself in a military hospital with a broken collarbone, in the same month he wants to be a witness to the marriage of his brother Rudolf.

He always has his way. On 31 August he is standing in front of the door in Heidenreichstein on time and carries out his duties. His arm is in a cast for two days until he must return to the military hospital in severe pain. As a reminder of this event a crooked shoulder remains. His fracture is hardly healed before he is released to the Front of his own free will.

Two pictures during his stay at the military hospital. With his mother on the balcony of the Viennese apartment (above), and or a stroll through town.

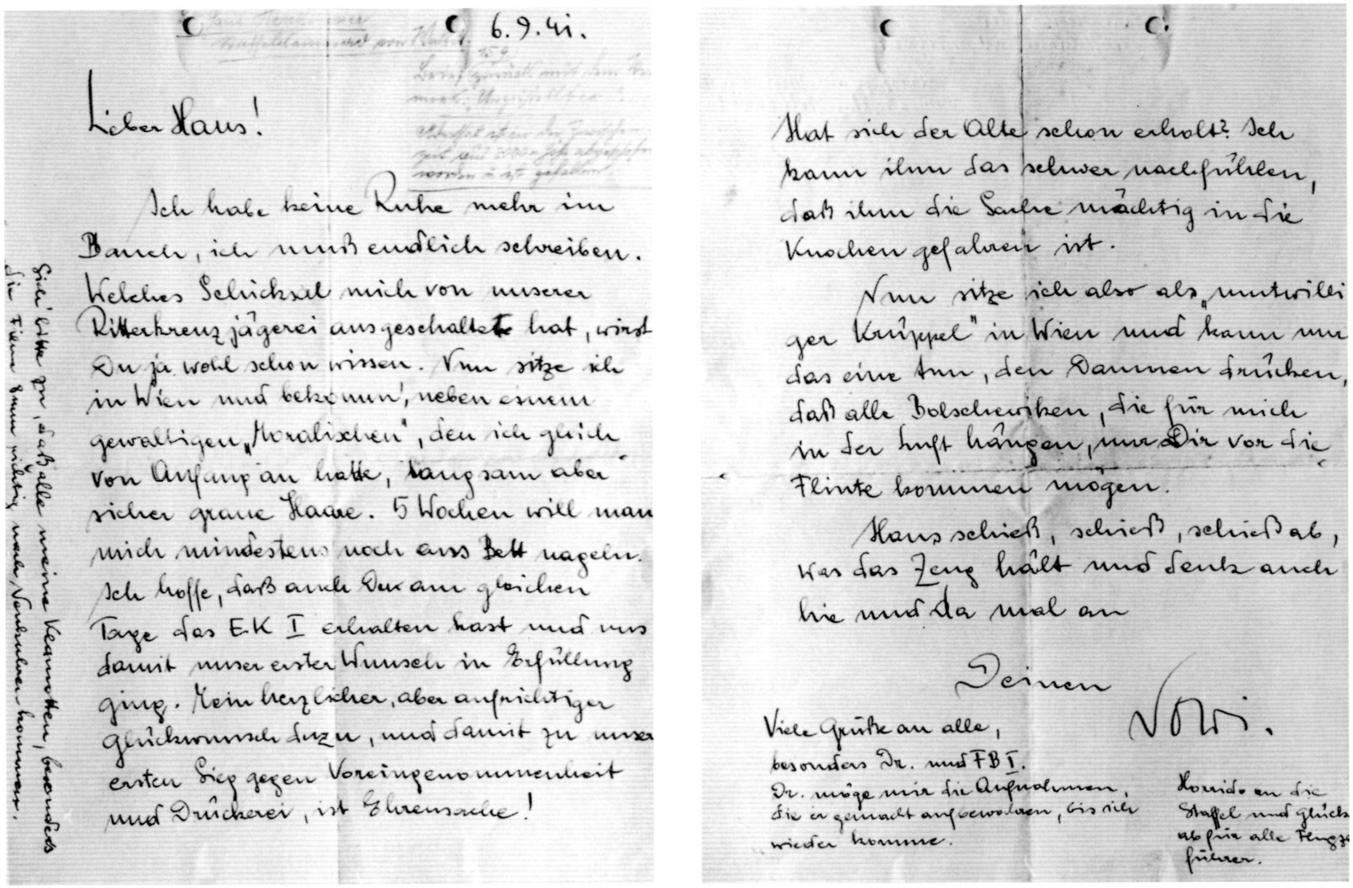

6.9.41.

Lieber Hans!

Ich habe keine Ruhe mehr im Bauch, ich muß endlich schreiben. Welches Schicksal mich von unserer Ritterkreuzjägerei ausgeschaltet hat, wirst Du ja wohl schon wissen. Nun sitze ich in Wien und bekomme, neben einem gewaltigen „Moralischen", den ich gleich von Anfang an hatte, langsam aber sicher graue Haare. 5 Wochen will man mich mindestens noch ans Bett nageln. Ich hoffe, daß auch Du am gleichen Tage das E.K I erhalten hast und uns damit unser erster Wunsch in Erfüllung ging. Mein herzlicher, aber aufrichtiger Glückwunsch dazu, und damit zu unserem ersten Sieg gegen Voreingenommenheit und Drückerei, ist Ehrensache!

Hat sich der Alte schon erholt? Ich kann ihm das schwer nachfühlen, daß ihm die Sache mächtig in die Knochen gefahren ist.

Nun sitze ich also als „unfreiwilliger Krüppel" in Wien und kann nur das eine tun, den Daumen drücken, daß alle Bolschewiken, die für mich in der Luft hängen, nur Dir vor die Flinte kommen mögen.

Hans schieß, schieß, schieß ab, was das Zeug hält und denk auch hie und da mal an

Deinen

Nowi.

Viele Grüße an alle, besonders Dr. und FB I. Dr. möge mir die Aufnahmen, die er gemacht aufbewahren, bis ich wieder komme.

Horrido an die Staffel und Glück ab für alle Flugzeugführer.

Letter to his friend *Leutnant* Henkemeier on September 6, 1941.

After the occupation of Ösel by German troops a German JG 54 unit occupies this area (Autumn 1941).

Hans-Leopold Henkemeier, who is shot down above Ösel, finds his last place of rest in a German military cemetery. The remains of his plane lay in an area of the forest. Right picture: the tail with holes that mark the shots.

The Russian winter that suddenly in 1941/42 sets in comes as a surprise to the German units. The men of the ground crew achieve the superhuman when it comes to having the planes ready.

Left: A Bf 109 after a belly landing in a mission over the Newa. The pilot brings his plane back to the air despite hard hits from anti-aircraft artillery.
Right: Pilots of *Ergänzungsgruppe* JG 54 in Siverskaja during a meeting in November 1941. From the left: Döbele, Nowotny, Kretschmer, unknown, Hörmann, and unknown.

The groups of JG 54 spend the cold winter months of 1941/42 on the former Russian Siverskaja and Krasnowardeisk airports. For the ground crew it is easier to maintain the planes in the big, protective hangars. Nowotny is especially proud of the "men in black," because even in the most severe winter his plane is always ready for takeoff. He thanks them for it with his air victories.

The bearer of the *Ritterkreuz*, *Hauptmann* Franz Eckerle, is entrusted with the command of I. JG 54. Eckerle, who was a famous stunt pilot before the war, leads his unit with care from success to success. On February 14, 1942, he made a forced landing behind Russian lines because of an attack and has been missing since then. According to press reports Eckerle won 62 air victories. Later he is awarded with the *Eichenlaub*

Oberleutnant Wolfgang Späte, *Kapitän* of *5. Staffel*, is awarded with the *Ritterkreuz* after 45 air victories on October 5, 1941. The shot is taken in Winter 1941/42 in Staraja-Russa.

Aerial photograph of the Siverskaja airport. In the top left the shoveled runway is easily recognized.

After *Oberst* Werner Mölders' tragic death—the newly appointed *General der Jagdflieger*, Adolf Galland, visits the *Ostgeschwader* in winter 1941/42. Major Hannes Trautloft, the *Kommodore* of JG 54, receives his guest, and accompanies him to the combat post of the *Geschwader* in Siverskaja.

Gefreiter Schnörrer wins his first air victory on December 31, 1941. The *Schwarmführer* Horst Ademeit is less pleased than his comrades. Schnörrer voluntarily left the formation and attacked an opponent, which yields heavy punishment.

After the dissolution of the *Ergänzungs-Jagdgruppe*, the pilots of the three groups of the *Geschwader* are separated. *Lt.* Nowotny is assigned to *I. Gruppe* and flies under *Oblt.* Koall in *3. Staffel.* The Bf 109 flown by Nowotny in the "Grünes Herz" of JG 54 carries his personal lucky number 13.

3. Staffel is also stationed at the former Russian Krasnowardeist airport in Winter 1941/42. The men are accommodated in the palace of the former tsarina in Gatschina. The picture shows *Oblt.* Koall (white shirt and tie) in the circle of his pilots. Nowotny is in the back left without a cap.

The *Staffelkapitän* of 4./JG 54, *Hptm.* Hans Philipp, takes over *I. Gruppe* in February 1942. After 86 air victories Philipp is awarded with the *Eichenlaub mit Schwertern*. The *Kommandeur*'s achievements goad on the young pilots. In Philipp Nowotny finds his role model.

Verleihungsurkunde

Im Namen des
Oberbefehlshabers der Luftwaffe

verleihe ich dem

Leutnant Walter N o w o t n y

3./Jagdgeschwader 54

die

**Frontflug-Spange für Jäger
in Gold**

O.U., den 17.Mai 1942

Major und Geschwaderkommodor

The *Frontflugspange für Jäger in Gold* is awarded to *Lt.* Nowotny from 3./JG 54 on May 17, 1942.

The "Grünherz-Jäger" have their hands full at Wolchow. Nowotny and his new "Katschmarek" Schnörrer are called "Max and Moritz" by the *Landser*. Like eagles they push through the Russian *Schlachtflugzeug* formations and ease the burden in the sky for the military troops. The picture shows a comrade after a successful mission.

Schnörrer in his "Weifle 9" in front of Leningrad. He later remains true to the tactical number "Weifle 9" after the group was converted to Fw 190s.

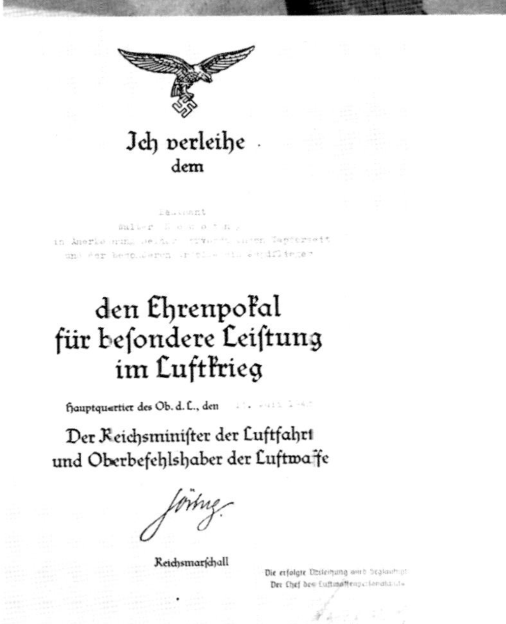

Ich verleihe
dem

den Ehrenpokal
für besondere Leistung
im Luftkrieg

Hauptquartier des Ob. d. L., den

Der Reichsminister der Luftfahrt
und Oberbefehlshaber der Luftwaffe

Reichsmarschall

On July 10, 1942, Nowotny achieves his 31st and 32nd air victories at Wolchow-Brückenkopf. He receives the *Ehrenpokal* for special achievements in air combat on July 14, 1942.

The bookkeeping on the tail is gladly shown to war correspondents. In combat the pilot is especially in danger. The upper picture displays the tail of the Bf 109F of the *Kommandeur* of *I. Gruppe*, *Hptm.* Philipp, in Siverskaja on March 31, 1942. The lower picture shows *Lt.* Nowotny's "Weifle 8."

Nr. im Jagdgeschw. Abt. 79078

40

17.7.42.

an: 24.7.
ab: 26.7.

Liebe Eltern!

Da wir nun schon seit einer Woche Schlechtwetter haben, bleibt mir auch mehr Zeit zum Schreiben. Wenn ich so zum Fenster hinausschaue, so ist es mir, als ob uns der Sommer hier oben schon wieder den Rücken zeigen wollte. Dauernd feucht, trübe und auch teilweise schon wieder kalt – Vorboten des Winters. Fliegen ist beinahe zur Feiertagsbeschäftigung geworden. Den einen Grund habe ich Euch im letzten Brief schon geschrieben, die Russen haben den größten Teil ihrer Luftwaffe nach dem Süden geworfen – ein zweiten für mich ebenso wenn nicht noch mehr, unangenehmer Grund oder besser gesagt – Mißgrund – ist das schlechte Wetter. Nur einmal, so gegen Ende voriger Woche, schien es, als ob die Russen bei uns hier etwas vor hätten. Mit einer Unmenge von Panzern, schweren und leichten Infantriewaffen, Artillerie und Spezialsturmtruppen rannten sie gegen einen unserer Wolchowbrückenköpfe an. Ich will fast sagen, zu meiner Freude – muß aber leider sagen, zum Leidwesen unserer Kameraden von der Infantrie setzten sie an 2-3 Tagen auch wieder ihre Luftwaffe ein. Da war wieder mal die Zeit für uns gekommen und wir haben mächtig reingehalten. 15 Stück haben wir (meine Staffel) dabei erledigt. Als höchste Anerkennung für uns kam – schöner als alle Orden – ein Dankschreiben der Infantrie, die unter den russ. Tiefangriffen und Bombeneinsätzen viel zu leiden hatte. Ich selbst habe dabei meinen 31. u. 3 Luftsieg errungen. Leider dauerte für uns der Kram nur 2-3 Tage, nun sind die russ. Flieger wieder K.O. und wir warten wieder – –. Anbei 2 Marken, mit denen bis zu 1000 g Pakete an die Front geschickt werden können. Herzliche Grüße an Hugo, Rosl und alle Bekannten.

Horrido! Euer Beni

Schickt mir bitte für nächsten Brief die Nummer von der Urkunde zu meinem goldenen K.J. Abzeichen.

Letter to his parents on July 17, 1942.

Nowotny is lucky things did not turn out worse with this "Rote 1" in summer 1942. After heavy air combat he must return prematurely to the air base because of canon hits. While he is gliding in for landing—the engine stalls—the plane scrapes the rampart of a flak and noses over. Only after twenty minutes can his comrades free him from the cabin. But this occurrence does not stop him from taking off with another Me 109 to battle the enemy.

On August 2, 1942, *Lt.* Nowotny defeats his seventh air opponent. It is the 48th to 54th air victory. His loyal men cheerfully greet him at his plane.

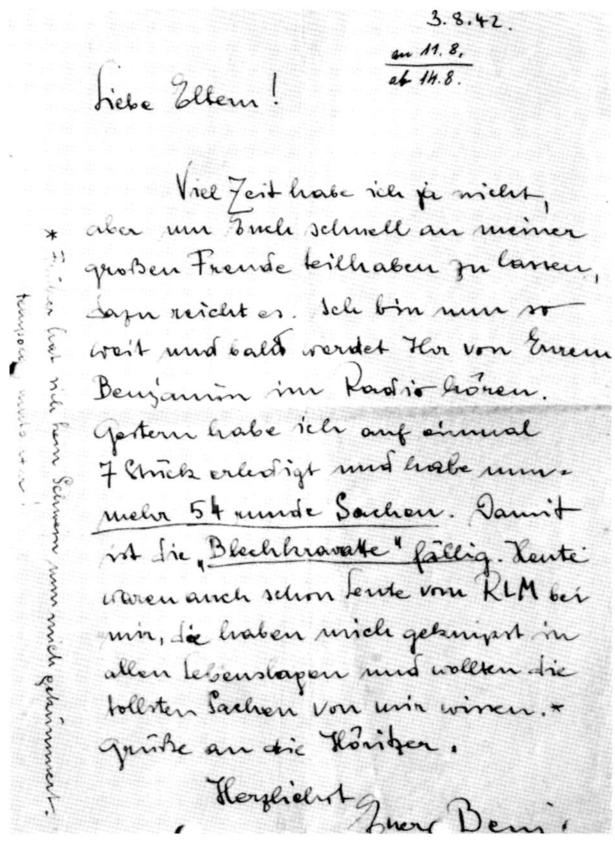

3.8.42.
an 11.8.
ab 14.8.

Liebe Eltern!

Viel Zeit habe ich ja nicht, aber um Euch schnell an meiner großen Freude teilhaben zu lassen, dazu reicht es. Ich bin nun so weit und bald werdet Ihr von Eurem Benjamin im Radio hören. Gestern habe ich auf einmal 7 Stück erledigt und habe nunmehr 54 runde Sachen. Damit ist die „Blechkravatte" fällig. Heute waren auch schon Leute vom RLM bei mir, sie haben mich geknipst in allen Lebenslagen und wollten die tollsten Sachen von mir wissen.* Grüße an die Höritzer.

Herzlichst Euer Beni.

* Früher hat sich kein Schwein um mich gekümmert.

Letter to his parents on August 3, 1942.

Vorläufiges Besitzzeugnis

Der Führer
und Oberste Befehlshaber
der Wehrmacht

hat

dem Leutnant Walter Nowotny

das Ritterkreuz
des Eisernen Kreuzes
am 4.Septemb.1942 verliehen.

Berlin, den 4. September 1942
Der Chef des Luftwaffenpersonalamts
I.V.

Generalmajor

Lt. Nowotny is awarded with the *Ritterkreuz zum Eisernen Kreuz* on September 4, 1942, after 56 air victories. In the officers' mess of the Gatschina Palace, the men of the ground crew organize a grand celebration. Among the guests are the *Kommandeur* of *I. Gruppe*, *Hptm*. Philipp, and *Hptm*. Haase (picture below). Top right: the bearer of the *Ritterkreuz* during the studying of press reports and congratulatory telegrams.

C'EST L'USAGE ALLEMAND D'ATTAQUER L'ADVERSAIRE DE FACE, ET DE LE TERRASSER EN COMBAT FRANC, ET NON PAS EN TRAÎTRE.

L'EMPEREUR HENRI II.

SCHWEICKHARDT — Capitaine SCHENCK — Lieutenant RALL

Adjudant-chef STOTZ — Adjudant-chef ZWERNEMANN

En hommage reconnaissant de leur activité héroique dans la lutte pour l'avenir de notre peuple, le Führer a décoré le Lieutenant Günther Rall dans une formation de chasse comme 134ème soldat, l'Adjudant-Chef Max Stotz, pilote dans une formation de chasse, à l'occasion de sa 100ème victoire comme 137ème soldat, le Capitaine Henri Schweickhardt, pilote dans une formation de bombardement comme 138ème soldat, le Capitaine Wolfgang Schenck pilote dans une formation de destroyers comme 139ème soldat, et l'Adjudant-Chef Joseph Zwernemann, pilote dans une formation de chasse à l'occasion de sa 101ème victoire comme 141ème soldat de l'armée allemande, de la

FEUILLE DE CHÊNE DE LA CROIX DE CHEVALIER DE LA CROIX DE FER

Lieutenant BARKHORN — Lieutenant BORNSCHEIN — Lieutenant NEMECEK — Sous-lieutenant HEMMER

COMMENT ILS ONT GAGNÉ LA CROIX DE CHEVALIER

Le Lieutenant Gérard Barkhorn, Chef d'escadrille dans une formation de chasse est un chasseur qui s'est distingué par son esprit de sacrifice exemplaire et par sa haute science aéronautique. A gagné 59 victoires aériennes. — Le Lieutenant Walter Bornschein, pilote dans une formation de bombardement fait partie des plus vieux pilotes particulièrement distingués de sa formation. Entre autres, dans des missions contre l'Angleterre il a jeté ses bombes au cours de nombreux vols de jour et de nuit sur des aérodromes, des usines, des docks et s'est distingué, lors d'attaques en rase-mottes sur des navires et des convois. — Le Lieutenant Ludovic Nemecek, observateur dans une escadrille de grande reconnaissance, et le Sous-lieutenant Hermann Hemmer, pilote dans une escadrille de grande reconnaissance forment un équipage qui uni par un étroit lien de camaraderie atteint des succés exceptionnels dans l'exécution des missions qui lui ont été confiées contre l'Angleterre. Attaqué 39 fois par des chasseurs anglais et mêlé à de trés sévères combats aériens, il a abattu 6 avions ainsi que deux saucisses. — L'exploit le plus marquant du Sous-lieutenant Conrad Hennemann, pilote dans une formation de bombardement, a été le coulage du croiseur lourd américain qui accompagnait le convoi géant anéanti dans l'océan Arctique par l'aviation et les soumarins allemands le 4 juillet 1942. Le vaillant Sous-lieutenant n'est pas revenu de cette mission. — Le Sous-lieutenant Walter Nowotny, pilote dans une formation de chasse, est un chasseur audacieux qui est sorti victorieux de 56 combats aériens avec des soviets. — L'Adjudant-chef Hans Schleef, pilote dans une formation de chasse a réussi au cours de plus de 200 vols d'abattre 41 avions. — L'Adjudant-chef Henri Klöpper, pilote dans une formation de chasse, a abbatu 66 avions ennemis

Photos de la PK des correspondants de guerre Röder (Sch 2), Jütte (Sch 1), Reimers (Sch 1), Strobel (Sch 1), Wanderer (Sch 1), Photos privées (2), Scherl-CKW (5)

Sous-lieutenant HENNEMANN † Sous-lieutenant NOWOTNY — Adjudant-chef SCHLEEF — Adjudant-chef KLÖPPER

Bearer of the *Ritterkreuz* Walter Nowotny.

The "Adler"—here the French propaganda edition—acknowledges the achievements of the new bearer of the *Ritterkreuz* (Nowotny lower left).

6. Staffel of JG 54 under *Oblt.* Sattig has an outcome to be proud of. Many pilots later receive the *Ritterkreuz*. In the picture from the left: *Uffz.* Fieber, *Fw.* Büchner, *Uffz.* Wolff, *Uffz.* Wernicke, *Fw.* Schleinhege, *Oblt.* Sattig, *Lt.* Beiflwenger, *Uffz.* Klopp, *Uffz.* Runge, and *Uffz.* Nickel. The *Kapitän* of the *Staffel*, Karl Sattig, is missing in the Rshew area since August 10, 1942. Later he is awarded with the *Ritterkreuz* on September 19, 1942, for his 53 air victories.

After the conferment of the *Ritterkreuz* Nowotny is due for leave. In Vienna—at his parents—the brothers Walter and Hubert meet for the last time. Hubert falls in Stalingrad.

Left: The *Kommodore* of the "Grünherzgeschwader," *Major* Hannes Trautloft, is shown laughing in his BF 109E "Emil." 500 missions are a reason to celebrate. In the "Grünes Herz" the coat of arms of his three groups. Right: the *Staffelkapitän* of 1./JG 54, *Oblt.* Heinz Lange, accepts a report from one of his *Schwarmführer*, *Ofw.* Horst Ademeit.

The *Kommodore* with his *Gruppenkommandeure*: left to right: Seiler, Hrabak, Trautloft, and Philipp.

On October 25, 1942, *Oblt.* Lange hands over 1. *Staffel* to Lt. Walter Nowotny. *Oblt.* Lange is being transferred to JG 51. In 1945 he is the last *Kommodore* of this *Geschwader.*

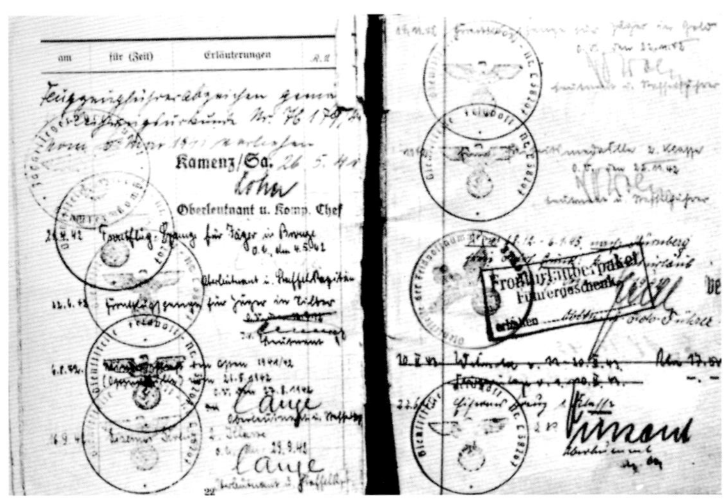

Entries of the *Staffelkapitäne* in Schnörrer's service record book.

Quarters of the *Geschwader* in Winter 1942/43 in Gatschina Palace.

The "Geschwaderbär" with the group's coat of arms at the entrance to the palace.

Snow storms and icy coldness in Winter 1942/43. The Me 109s are covered with tarps, and must often be shoveled free.

Despite the severe cold, there is no rest for the "Grünherz-Jäger." Max Stotz flies *Jabo*-missions with his *Staffel*. On the Front Russian *Panzerrudel* try to break down German positions. With two 250-kg bombs under the slim fuselage of their Me 109 the fighter pilots fly their mission.

In January 1943 the first JG 54 is converted to the new fighter plane Focke-Wulf Fw 190. Full of praise, the pilots take possession of this plane. The strong power of the engine, the high visibility from the cabin, and the wide undercarriage excite everyone.

Aerial photograph of the Krasnowardeisk airport. In the foreground the big hangars.The palace and their quarters are to the right behind the wooded area.

With the Fw 190 Lt. Nowotny achieves his 300th air victory in the *Staffel*—an event that should be well celebrated.

The Fw 190s of the *Gruppenadjutanten* taxi to takeoff. The interested ground crew follows the course of events.

I. Staffel in front of the new plane. Left of Nowotny is Anton Döbele, and behind them Rudolf Rademacher. To the far left is Schnörrer.

Nowotny discusses the mission with Döbele. The planes are standing at the edge of the area in the splitter boxes that are covered with camouflage netting. During this miss on Nowotny flies "Weifle 10."

With a parachute the *Leutnant* climbs into the cabin of the Focke-Wulf, and soon the motor is running and warming up.

Right: Schnörrer goes through a *Werkstattflug*. The plane glides into a landing with fully beaten landing flaps.

"Weifle 9" touches down softly and taxis into the box.

The new *Kommandeur* of *II. Gruppe*, Major Hans "Assi" Hahn, initiated himself well into JG 54. On January 26, 1943, he celebrates his 100th air victory. Max Stotz defeats his 150th enemy on the same day. *Oblt.* Hand Beiflwenger, who is situated in between with his air victories, celebrates as well. "Assi" Hahn must make a forced landing behind Russian lines in Demjansk due to engine trouble, and is taken prisoner on February 21, 1943. Beiflwenger has been missing since March 6, 1943, in the Ilmensee area after air combat with ten enemy fighter pilots. Stotz is shot down by Witebsk on August 19, 1943, and is missing, as well. A tragic outcome.

On February 1, 1943, Walter Nowotny is promoted to *Oberleutnant*. For the *Kapitän* of *1. Staffel* an especially successful time begins. The famous *Schwarm*—Nowotny, Döbele, Rademacher, and Schnörrer—win battle after battle. In the quarters of the Palace Gatschina many real skat duels take place. Döbele, Swabian by birth, does not miss an opportunity for this.

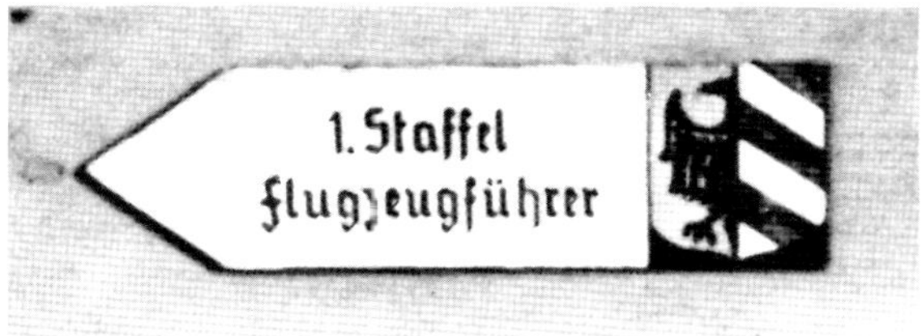

The *Staffel*'s Focke-Wulf Fw 190 is painted white during the winter months. Nowotny, together with Döbele, takes off for a mission. The Russian *Schlachtflugzeuge* attack the German infantry positions, and action must be taken. On March 16, 1943, in the Staraja-Russa area the young *Oberleutnant* wins four further air victories: numbers 69 to 72.

The planes are placed in the splitter box warm-up, and then taxi to the start on the shoveled runway.

Left: The days of the *Kommandeur* of I./JG 54 are numbered in the troop. On March 17, 1943, he defeats his 200th air opponent with his Fw 190. On April 1, 1943, he takes over JG 1 in the west as *Kommodore*.

An *Unteroffizier* of the *Staffel* is responsible for the mission overview. At a glance it is recognized which plane is in a mission or in the hangar for repairs.

This shot clearly illustrates the difficulties that the Russian winter brings to air traffic. Russian prisoners of war are sent to clear the airfield. Runways must be cleared to hangars and boxes.

Slowly it becomes spring. The *Staffeln* transfer—according to need—to other areas. In Sagan, the accommodations of the pilots carry the name "Haus Nowotny." The *Fähnriche* Sepp Quada and Adolf Lanzenbacher chat. The runway transforms into a field of mud. The planes get an extensive camouflage painting.

"Weifle 1" taxis out of the splitter box to takeoff.

Schnörrer's "Weifle 9" was hit by flak at Emga. That was a close one. Nowotny is glad that his friend succeeded in bringing back the plane to the air base despite it.

Lt. Horst Hanning and *Lt.* Kretschmer from *5. Staffel* during "Liegestuhl-Sitzbereitschaft,' in Rjelbizi. Hannig defeats 90 opponents in the east, and is transferred at the beginning of 1943 as *Staffelführer* to JG "Richthofen" No. 2 on the channel. On May 15, 1943, he falls in Caen in an air battle with Spitfire-*Jäger*.

Oblt. Nowotny wins his 82nd air victory in the meantime. On May 20, 1943, this maneuverable "Rata" flies through his *MG-Garben*. The Russian pilot manages a nice belly landing.

The famous *Schwarm*, *Oblt*. Nowotny and his men: from the left: Döbele, Schnörrer, and Rademacher. Together they win their 524th air victory, but only Rademacher and Schnörrer survive the war.

The pennant of I./JG 54. Left the chimney sweep, the Staffel coat of arms, and right the coat of arms of I./JG 54. The shot of the pennant must have been taken in Rjelbizi. The dark stripes of the pennant bear the until now mission havens of the *Staffel*.

At the end of March 1943 Major Hans Philipp left his *I. Gruppe* to take over JG 1—already a *Geschwader* of the *Reichsverteidigung*. Hannes Trautloft, the *Kommodore* of JG 54, landed with the *Fieseler* "Storch," in order to depart from his *Gruppenkommandeur*. In the picture from the right: Trautloft, *Hptm*. Koall (3. *Staffel*), *Oblt*. Nowotny (1. *Staffel*)—half covered: *Oblt*. Dutel (Adj. I./JG 54).

The group is lined up for departure. From the left: *Oblt*. Nowotny, *Lt*. Teumer, *Lt*. Loos, *Hptm*. Wettstein, and pilots of *I. Gruppe*.

Major Philipp left the eastern theater of war on board a Ju 52. The officer and pilot had to soon recognize how difficult the missions of the fighter pilots in the *Reichsverteidigung* are. The battle against the *:bermacht* of the Allies in the West—heavily armed *Bomberpulks* with protective *Jägerschwärme*—call for a completely different method of fighting. On October 8, 1943, Hans Philipp fails in air combat with "Thunderbolt"-*Jägern*.

The next nine pictures illustrate *Oblt.* Nowotny's mission against Russian SB-2 Bombers in sequential order.

Nowctny flies with "Weifle 5."

Attacking from a high altitude, the German fighter pilot's weapons meet the opponent's fuel tanks. The bomber's smoke trail shows the solders of the *Waffen-SS* that they are safe from this opponent.

Nowotny flies in a swerving motion over the airfield and announces a new air victory. The joy is great. The men of the ground crew take charge of the Focke-Wulf and prepare it for the next mission.

A happy return home. Despite the heavy hits in the rudder assembly, a pilot of *1. Staffel* succeeds in the return flight and landing on the airfield. Nowotny reports on the mission.

Pilots of *5. Staffel* on the way to a meeting. The group combat post of II./JG 54 is set up in a straw-covered farmhouse in Rjelbizi.

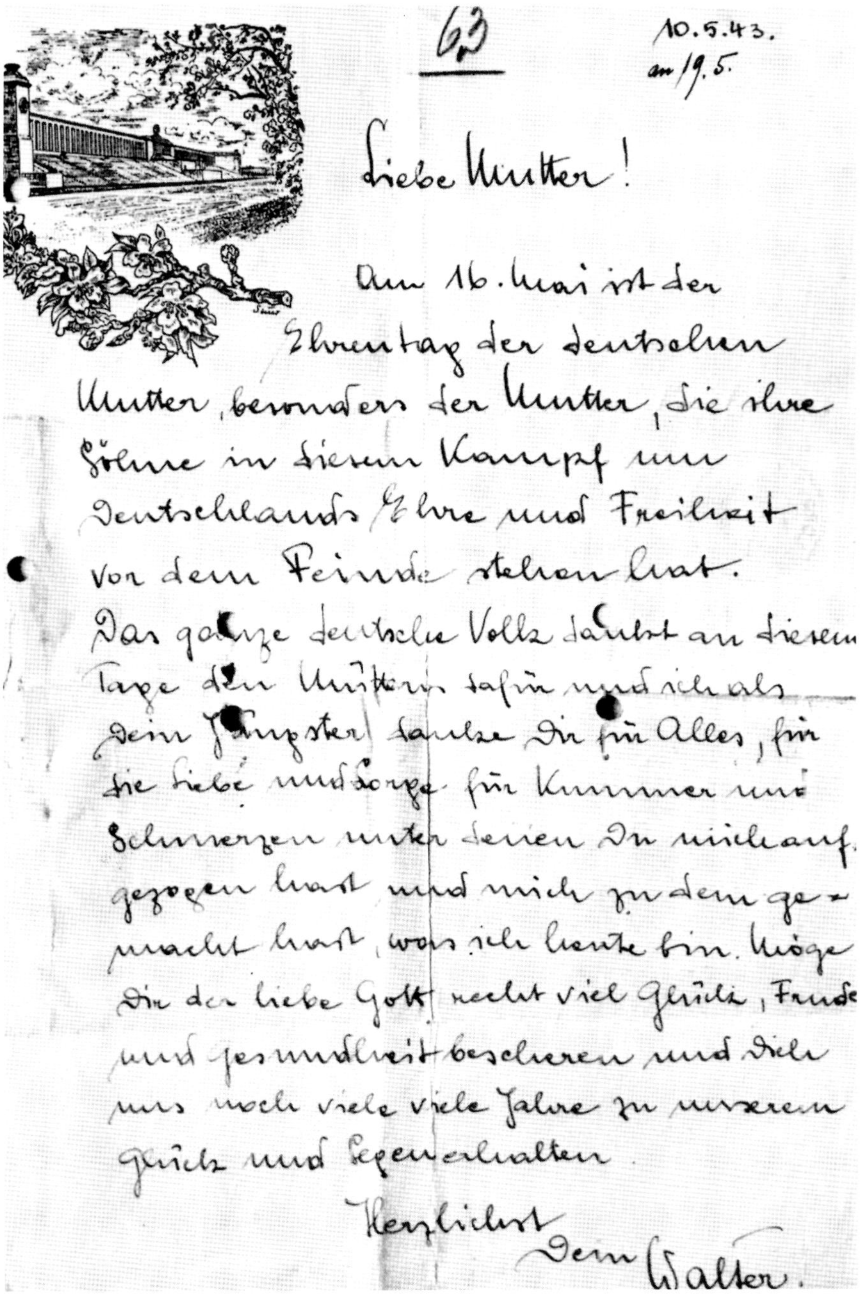

63

10.5.43.
an 19.5.

Liebe Mutter!

Am 16. Mai ist der Ehrentag der deutschen Mutter, besonders der Mutter, die ihre Söhne in diesem Kampf um Deutschlands Ehre und Freiheit vor dem Feinde stehen hat. Das ganze deutsche Volk dankt an diesem Tage den Müttern dafür und ich als Dein Jüngster danke Dir für Alles, für die Liebe und Sorge, für Kummer und Schmerzen unter denen Du mich aufgezogen hast und mich zu dem gemacht hast, was ich heute bin. Möge Dir der liebe Gott recht viel Glück, Freude und Gesundheit bescheren und Dich uns noch viele viele Jahre zu unserem Glück und Segen erhalten.

Herzlichst
Dein Walter.

With heartfelt words of thanks Walter Nowotny remembers his mother in Vienna. The close relationship between the "Benjamin" of the Nowotny family and the mother is stated in these lines. Walter never forgot a Mother's Day. The letter and picture are proof of it.

Always when the three *Staffeln* of *I. Gruppe* are on an airfield, the opportunity is seized to exchange experiences. In the picture from the left: *Oblt.* Robert Weifl, Otto Vinzent *Oblt.* Nowotny, and Erz, the group dentist.

Nowotny in a conversation with his Austrian compatriot *Oblt.* Robert Weifl, "Bazi." Since summer 1942, with the appointment to 3./JG 54 in the east, he already after a short time was rising to the top of the *Geschwader*. On March 26, 1944, he takes command of III./JG 54. After 121 air victories he falls in the west on December 29, 1944.

Exhaustingly Nowotny reports to his men on the survived air combat. The Fw 190 that he flew carries the name "Rammbock."

The face of the fighter plane Focke-Wulf Fw 190. With planes of this type Walter Nowotny has much success. He commands them like no other. The strength of the Fw 190 lies in the altitude range under 4000 meters, an ideal plane for the mission on the Eastern Front. Nowotny takes advantage of the benefits and possibilities of the plane. The powerful, robust engine, strong arms, good visibility from the cabin, and the wide undercarriage result in optimal requirements for fighter combat on the Eastern Front.

Hannes Trautloft—the *Kommodore* of the *Geschwader*—comes in the middle of May for an inspection of the *Gruppe*. The experienced Major Reinhard Seiler took over this group after the transfer of Hans Philipp to JG 1. The right picture shows *Oblt.* Nowotny in a conversation with the *Kommodore* before his takeoff.

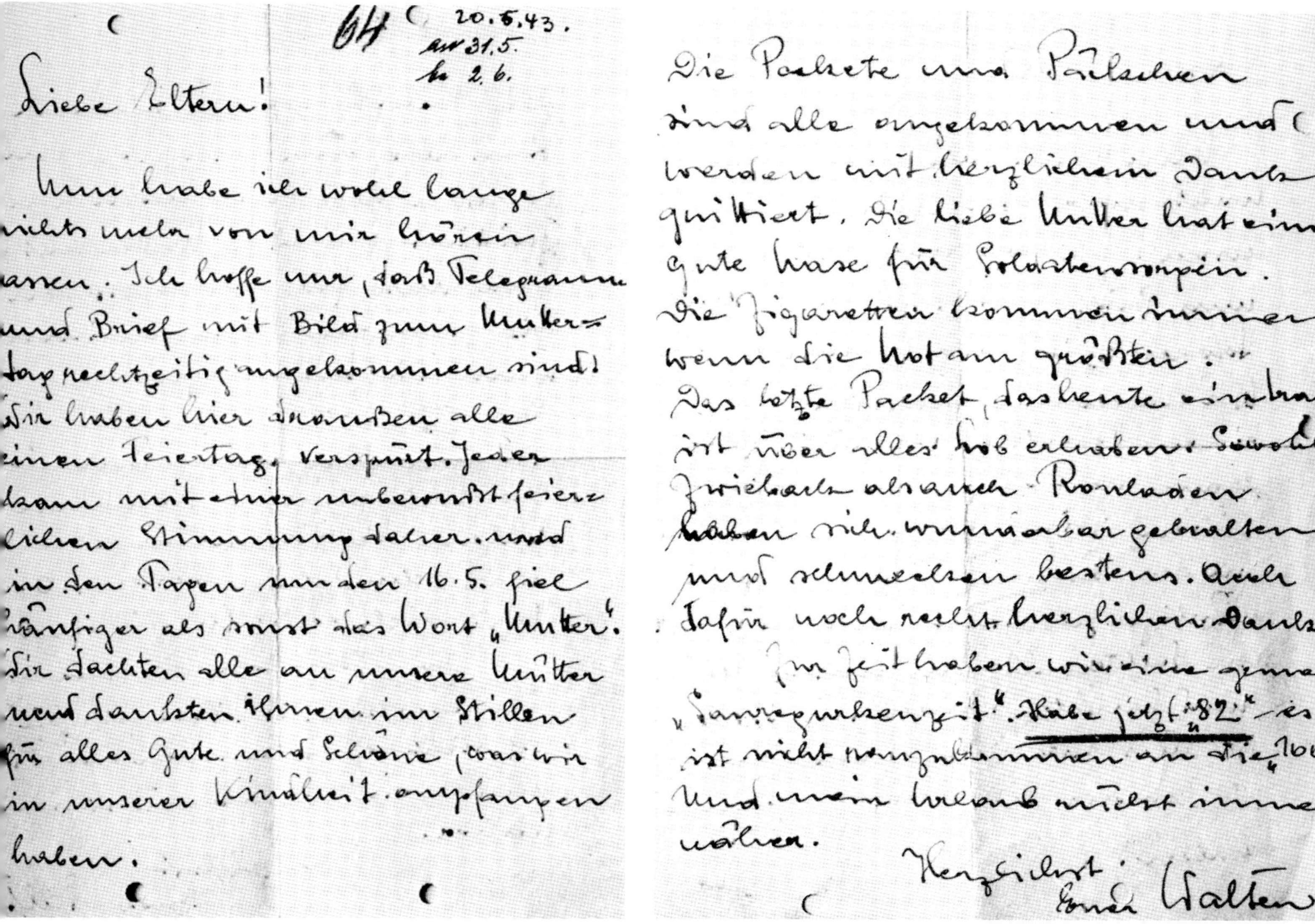

64 20.5.43.
an 31.5.
b 2.6.

Liebe Eltern!

Nun habe ich wohl lange nichts mehr von mir hören lassen. Ich hoffe nur, daß Telegramm und Brief mit Bild zum Muttertag rechtzeitig angekommen sind! Wir haben hier draußen alle einen Feiertag verspürt. Jeder kam mit einer unbewußt feierlichen Stimmung daher und in den Tagen um den 16.5. fiel häufiger als sonst das Wort „Mutter". Wir dachten alle an unsere Mütter und dankten Ihnen im Stillen für alles Gute und Schöne, was wir in unserer Kindheit empfangen haben.

Die Packete und Päckchen sind alle angekommen und werden mit herzlichem Dank quittiert. Die liebe Mutter hat eine gute Nase für Soldatenwünsche. Die Zigaretten kommen immer wenn die Not am größten. Das letzte Packet, das heute eintraf ist über alles Lob erhaben. Sowohl Zwieback als auch Rouladen haben sich wunderbar gehalten und schmecken bestens. Auch dafür noch recht herzlichen Dank.

Zur Zeit haben wir eine genaue „Sauregurkenzeit". Habe jetzt „82" es ist nicht ganz gekommen an die „100" Und mein Urlaub nicht immer währen.

Herzlichst
Euer Walter

Letter to his parents on May 20, 1943.

Four men in a car. The "boss" is at the wheel again. Heino Cordes (with EK I) and *Fw.* Brehmer in the back seat.

"This is how your Willi lives in the field." Break time. Nowotny in a conversation with the group doctor, Dr. Vossberg.

On June 5, 1943, it has finally happened. Nowotny can enter his 100th air victory during his 344th mission into the books. He has reached the magic number 100. The ground crew honors their *Oberleutnant* with a *Eichensiegerkranz*. The air combat took place in Nowa-Lodoga. To the lower right the *Kapitän* of *3. Staffel*, Oblt. Franz Eisenach, congratulates Nowotny for his 100th air victory. Eisenach can enter his 100th air victory in the books on September 14, 1944, and receives the *Ritterkreuz* on October 10, 1944, as well.

Begleitschutz for bombers. This is also "hard bread" for the fighter pilots on the Eastern Front. The following, shortened report of events of a bomber pilot's crew should here stand on behalf of the many missions that Nowotny flew with his comrades.

Report of events (extracts) of the mission of the crew KG 53, AL + FA, on June 21, 1943, against the *Wolchowbrücken*, with forced landing in front of the main fighting line.

Crew of the AL + FA

Pilot:	*Ofw.* Kemmer
Sniper:	*Obltn.* Baake (Einsatzoffizier of KG 53)
Observer:	*Fw.* Stamm
Radio Operator:	*Fw.* Schmitz
Flight Mechanic:	*Uffz.* Benkendorf

The combat order states: The AL + FA flies into the unit of III. KG 53 and attacks the bridge 41325. The main focus is the middle part of the old section of the bridge that is still standing. The pickup of the *Jagdschutz* at an altitude of 6700 m above Sieverskaja, pickup time and departure from Sieverskaja at 19:33.

Time of attack: 20:00, one minute after the attack of I/53 on the anti-aircraft positions.
Arrival: Sieverskaja/Tossno-See in QU. 1042/-Pupyschevo-Ziel.
Altitude of attack: 6700-7000 m.

Takeoff took place in Korowje Selo at 18:10. Sieverkaja was departed from the landing course with *Jagdschutz* at 19:40 with continued climbing. During departure the unit counted 12 He 111s. The plane reached Wolchow's outermost flak zone at 20:15. The target itself was obscured from our Front overflight. At 20:00 I/53 attacked the flak position. Before reaching the flak zone the unit leader ordered the attack of the main target through BzB. After the flak zeroed in on the altitude and direction of the first planes the AL + FA was bombarded. At approximately 20:17 the plane received three direct hits, one in the cockpit through the *Lotfernrohr-Bombenvisiere* (*Lotfe*), and one in each motor. As a result of the hit in the *Lotfe* the observer's forearm was shattered. In the left motor the carburetor throttle controls or the fuel pipe were probably shot. The engine broke down immediately after the initial fire. The oil tank in the right motor was shot and broke down, as well, after 3 to 4 minutes. Immediately after the hit the observer threw the bombs from the *Notzug*, and the pilot tried to initiate a right turn. Because of the hit from the flak the tail unit was considerably damaged, and most of the surface was torn to shreds. The plane was forced into a left turn due to heavy pressing and a slanting. Because of this the plane lost 1000 m in altitude... The pilot tried to come to their lines by the shortest way possible. The right engine began to burn heavily. The plane fell at approximately 10 m per second. The return flight was made especially difficult due to a steady push of the plane to the right to *Ladogasse*. The cause of the right engine's failure, that was still running on idle, was largely due to the breaking action of the engine. It took all the physical strength and the help of other crew members to force the plane back on course...

At approximately an altitude of 700 m the burning engine fell apart. Only the crankshaft remained. The falling off of the engine gave the plane a favorable gliding angel (7m/sec) that made it possible for the pilot, as it later turned out, to overcome the 2.2 km. The pilot decided to carry out a forced landing on a marshland situated to the front left. During the Front overflight of the northeastern lined timber forest the plane was under attack by enemy infantry. The plane received many shots. During this attack the pilot touched down smoothly in a forced landing.

Because the plane was under attack, and there was a threat of detonation, the crew left the plane as quickly as possible with support for the injured. During the entire flight back the *Jagdgeschwader* Trautloft accompanied us in exemplary comradeship through all flaks, and made enemy fighter attacks impossible. After the forced landing the six *Jäger* held down the enemy infantry with their aircraft weapons above the area until it could be recognized from above that the crew was rescued. After *Weifl-Schieflen* of their own troops they flew away.

In a letter from the Front Nowotny reports to his parents about it, and ended with the sentence:

"Rarely was I so relieved, and rarely have I been so happy as in this moment, as all five men disappeared into the German trenches."

In July 1943 JG 54 receives a new *Kommodore, Major* Hubertus von Bonin. Hannes Trautloft becomes *Inspizient Ost* in the staff of the *General der Jagdflieger* (Galland). The pictures show Nowotny and *Lt.* Bernard Loos with the new *Kommodore* in the middle. Lower picture: a meeting with v. Bonin.

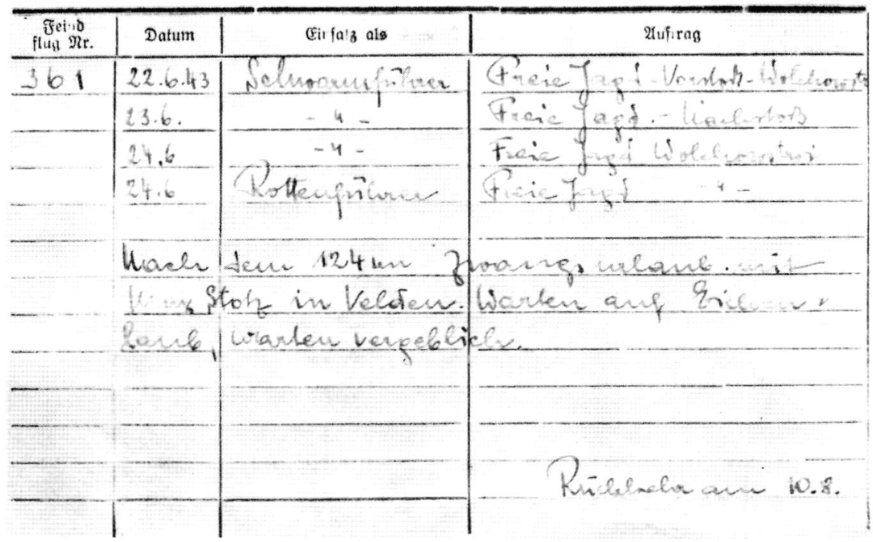

Feind flug Nr.	Datum	Einsatz als	Auftrag
361	22.6.43	Schwarmführer	Freie Jagd [illegible]
	23.6.	-"-	Freie Jagd [illegible]
	24.6	-"-	Freie Jagd [illegible]
	24.6	Rottenführer	Freie Jagd -"-
	Nach	dem 124ten	Zwangsurlaub mit
	Max Stotz in Velden.		Warten auf Eichen-
	laub,	warten vergeblich.	
			Rückkehr am 10.8.

On June 24, 1943, Walter Nowotny achieves his 124th air victory. In nine days 24 opponents were defeated! He goes with Max Stotz on leave to Velden. In his book of flight achievements we find the entry: "...Waiting for *Eichenlaub*, waiting in vain."

Hauptmann Max Stotz, also an Austrian compatriot of Nowotny, celebrates his 500th mission during this time. Stotz is *Kapitän* of 5./JG 54. On August 10, 1943, Nowotny and Stotz return to their unit after their leave. On August 19, 1943, Stotz is shot down in air combat by Witebsk. He bales out with a parachute behind Russian lines and has been missing since then. *Hptm.* Stotz defeated 189 opponents until his luck also ran out.

This shot was taken between 10 August and August 19, 1943. Trautloft visits his former *Geschwader* with *Gauleiter* Loose. From the left: *Oblt.* Rudorffer, *Hptm.* Stotz, Loose, *Oberstlt.* Trautloff, *Oblt.* Ademeit, *Hptm.* Seiler, *Oblt.* Nowotny, and *Hptm.* Götz.

Left: *Hptm.* Reinhard Seiler, who is the *Kommandeur* of *I. Gruppe* since May 1943, wins his 100th air victory. Seiler led III./JG earlier. In the middle of August 1943 he is badly injured, and remains unfit for service. Despite that, he takes over the *Schul-Jagdgeschwader* 104 as *Kommodore* in August 1944. Right: *Oblt.* Erich Rudorffer takes over II./JG 54 on August 1, 1943. Rudorffer came from JG 2 from the Western Front, where he won 74 air victories. Until October 28, 1944, he wins 136 more on the Eastern Front. As *Kommandeur* of II./JG 7—with the Me 262—he manages 12 air victories once again, 10 of which were bombers. Rudorffer experienced the end of the war with 222 air victories. On January 25, 1944, he is awarded with the *Schwerter zum Ritterkreuz des Eisernen Kreuzes*.

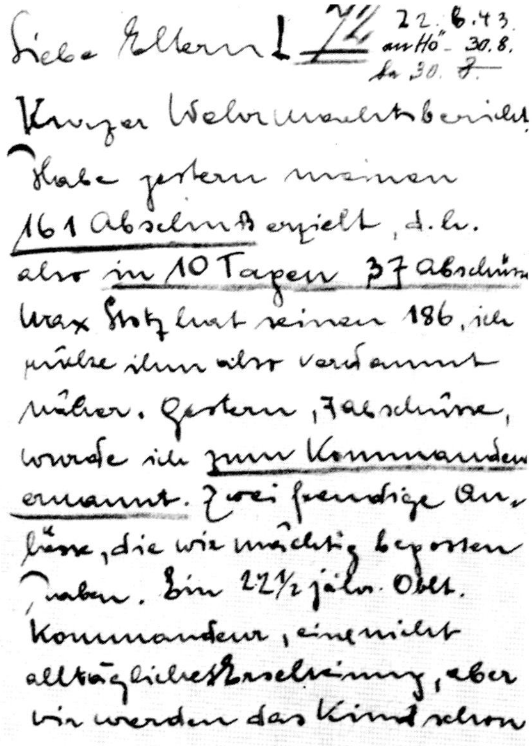

Liebe Eltern! 74 22.8.43. an Hö 30.8. ... 30.8.

Kurzer Wehrmachtsbericht: Habe gestern meinen 161 Abschuß erzielt, d.h. also in 10 Tagen 37 Abschüsse. Max Stotz hat seinen 186, ich rücke ihm also verdammt näher. Gestern, 7 Abschüsse, wurde ich zum Kommandeur ernannt. Zwei freudige Anlässe, die wir mächtig begossen haben. Ein 22½ jähr. Oblt. Kommandeur, eine nicht alltägliche Erscheinung, aber wir werden das Kind schon

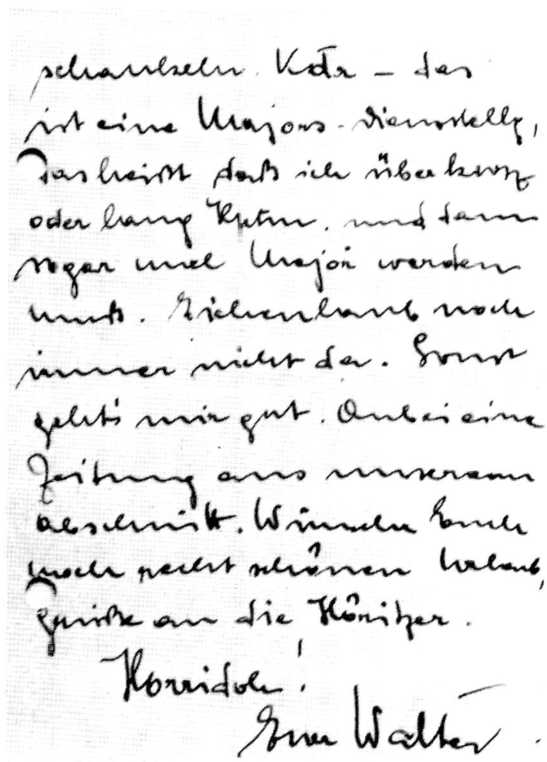

schaukeln. Kotz – das ist eine Majors-Dienststelle, das heißt daß ich über kurz oder lang Hptm. und dann sogar noch Major werden muß. Fliegerlaub noch immer nicht da. Sonst geht's mir gut. Anbei eine Zeitung aus unserem Abschnitt. Wünsche Euch noch recht schönen Urlaub, Grüße an die Könitzer.

Horrido!

Euer Walter.

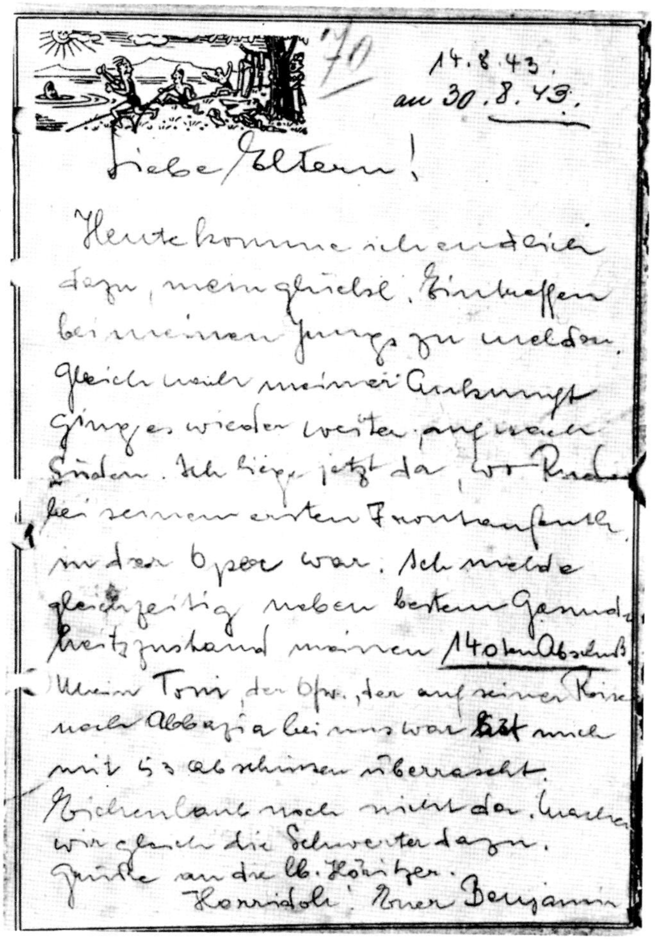

70 14.8.43. an 30.8.43.

Liebe Eltern!

Heute komme ich endlich dazu, mein glückl. Eintreffen bei meinen Jungs zu melden. Gleich nach meiner Ankunft ging es wieder weiter auf nach Süden. Ich liege jetzt da, wo Rudi bei seinem ersten Frontaufenthalt in der [illegible] war. Ich melde gleichzeitig neben bestem Gesundheitszustand meinen 140ten Abschuß. Mein Toni, der Ofw., der auf seiner Reise nach Abbazia bei uns war, hat mich mit 53 Abschüssen überrascht. Fliegerlaub noch nicht da. Machen wir gleich die Schwerter dazu. Grüße an die lb. Könitzer.

Horrido! Euer Benjamin

Both of the short notes to his parents describe the general condition of the situation on the Eastern Front. Little time remains for the fighter pilots to think of their families at home. The Russian Front is starting to move towards the west. The German fighter pilots become the "Feuerwehr." Nowotny's missions accumulate. The success of air victories increases by leaps and bounds in just a few days.

In his notes from August 22, 1943, Nowotny reports to his parents that he was put in charge of *I. Gruppe* a few days earlier. Pride speaks from these few lines. But there is no time to rest on his laurels. The number of air victories in August 1943 show what has taken place in the skies above the wavering German front:

8/12	125th - 128th air victory
8/13	129th - 137th air victory
8/14	138th - 140th air victory
8/15	141st air victory
8/18	150th air victory
8/21	155th - 161st air victory
9/1	174th - 183rd air victory

(News and dates were taken from the *Wehrmachtsbericht* and press reports.)

The *Kommandeur* of *I. Gruppe*, *Oberleutnant* Nowotny, reports to the *Kommodore* of JG 54, *Major* v. Bonin, on the strength of his unit in missions.

Like a burning torch, a Russian SB 2 bomber crashes to the ground.

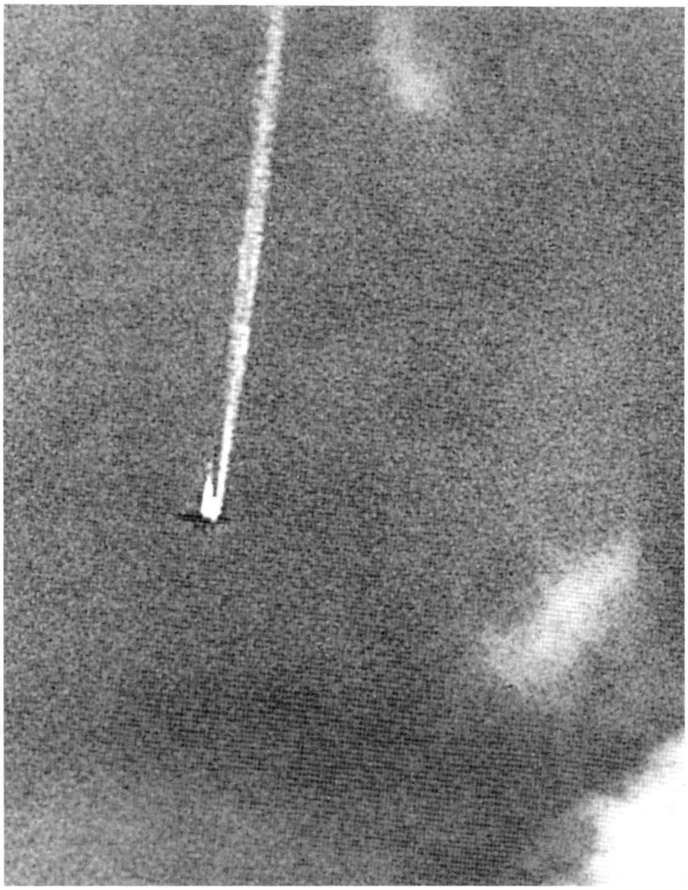

The head of *Luftflotte* 6, *Generaloberst* Robert Ritter von Greim, observes the mission of Nowotny's *Schwarm* with officers of his staff.

On the airfield of the *Gruppe* they became used to seeing the young *Kommandeur* sweeping over the grass runway in a swerving motion. The bearer of the *Eichenlaub* and *Kommandeur* of III./St.G. 2 "Immelmann," *Oberstlt*. Gustav Pressler, arrives to greet him. War reporter *Oblt*. Hübner (left) also congratulates the successful pilot.

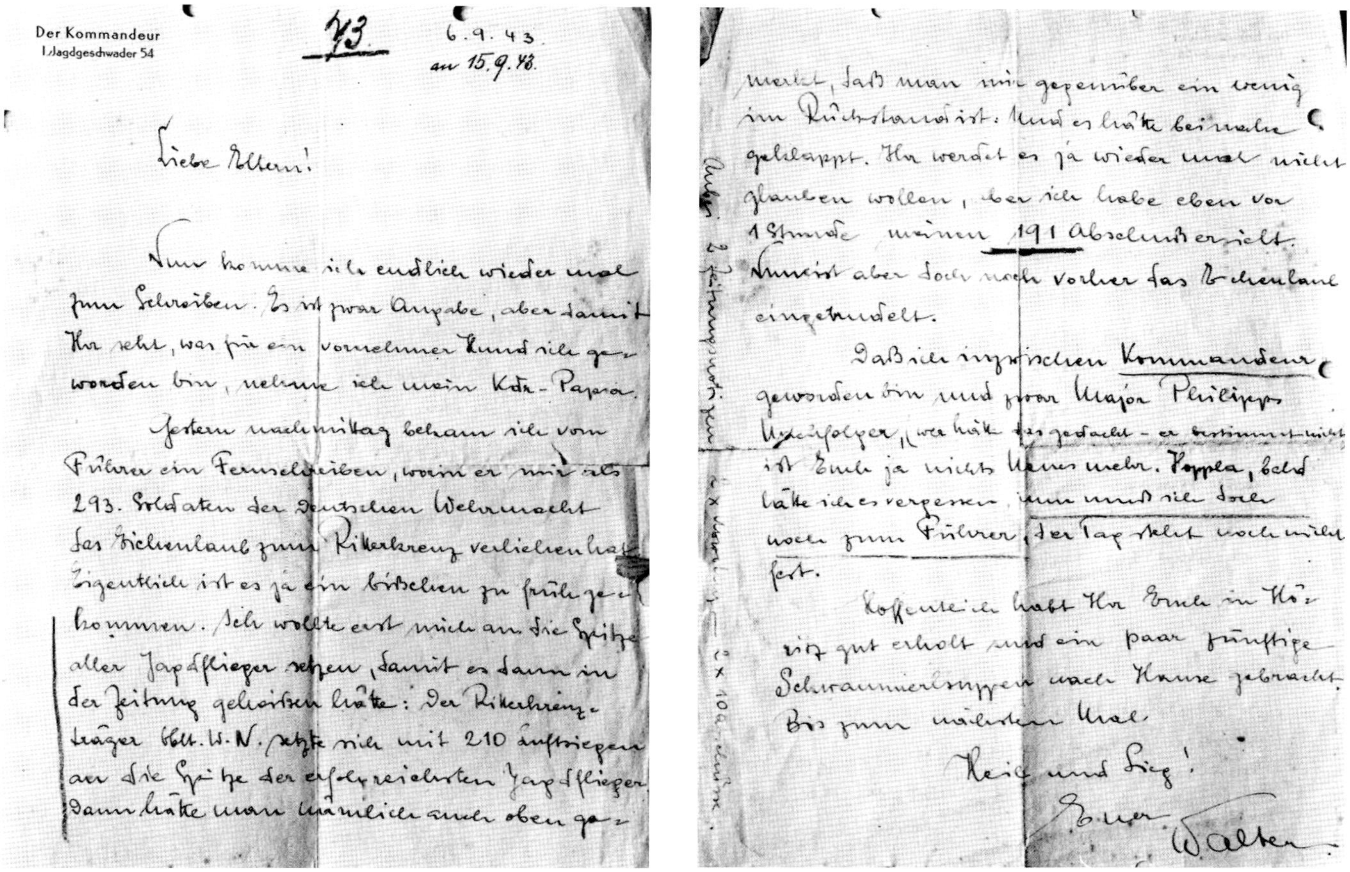

Der Kommandeur
I./Jagdgeschwader 54

43. 6.9.43.
an 15.9.43.

Liebe Eltern!

Nun komme ich endlich wieder mal zum Schreiben. Es ist zwar Angabe, aber damit Ihr seht, was für ein vornehmer Hund ich geworden bin, nehme ich mein Kdr.-Papier.

Gestern nachmittag bekam ich vom Führer ein Fernschreiben, worin er mir als 293. Soldaten der Deutschen Wehrmacht das Eichenlaub zum Ritterkreuz verliehen hat. Eigentlich ist es ja ein bißchen zu früh gekommen. Ich wollte erst mich an die Spitze aller Jagdflieger setzen, damit es dann in der Zeitung geheißen hätte: Der Ritterkreuzträger Oblt. W.N. setzte sich mit 210 Luftsiegen an die Spitze der erfolgreichsten Jagdflieger. Dann hätte man nämlich auch oben gemerkt, daß man mir gegenüber ein wenig im Rückstand ist. Und es hätte beinahe geklappt. Ihr werdet es ja wieder mal nicht glauben wollen, aber ich habe eben vor 1 Stunde meinen 191 Abschuß erzielt. Nun ist aber doch noch vorher das Eichenlaub eingetrudelt.

Daß ich inzwischen Kommandeur geworden bin und zwar Major Philipps Nachfolger, – wer hätte das gedacht – er bestimmt nicht – ist Euch ja nichts Neues mehr. Poppa, bald hätte ich es vergessen, nun muß ich doch noch zum Führer, der Tag steht noch nicht fest.

Hoffentlich habt Ihr Euch in Kö-[illegible] gut erholt und ein paar zünftige Schwammerlsuppen nach Hause gebracht. Bis zum nächsten Mal.

Heil und Sieg!

Euer Walter.

Letter to his parents on September 6, 1943.

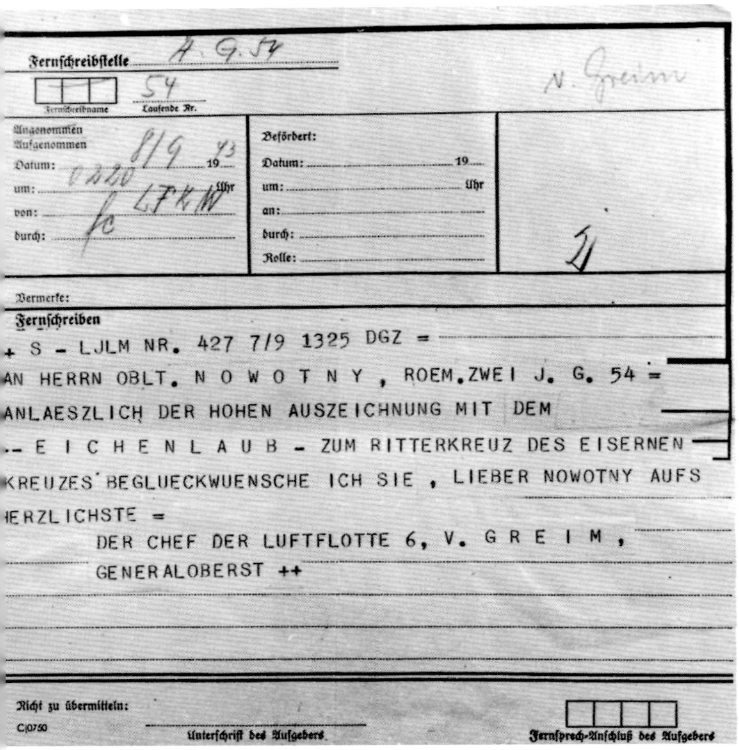

Fernschreibstelle A. G. 54

Fernschreibname 54 Laufende Nr.

n. Greim

Angenommen Aufgenommen
Datum: 8/9 19 43
um: 0220 Uhr
von: LFKW
durch: fc

Befördert:
Datum: 19
um: Uhr
an:
durch:
Rolle:

Vermerke:

Fernschreiben

\+ S - LJLM NR. 427 7/9 1325 DGZ =
AN HERRN OBLT. N O W O T N Y , ROEM.ZWEI J. G. 54 =
ANLAESZLICH DER HOHEN AUSZEICHNUNG MIT DEM
.- E I C H E N L A U B - ZUM RITTERKREUZ DES EISERNEN
KREUZES BEGLUECKWUENSCHE ICH SIE , LIEBER NOWOTNY AUFS
HERZLICHSTE =
DER CHEF DER LUFTFLOTTE 6, V. G R E I M ,
GENERALOBERST ++

Nicht zu übermitteln:
C 0750 Unterschrift des Aufgebers Fernsprech-Anschluß des Aufgebers

A congratulatory telegram on the awarding of the *Eichenlaub* from the head of *Luftflotte* 6, Ritter von Greim.

Major GRASSER

Hauptm. Prinz zu SAYN-WITTGENSTEIN

Oberleutnant ETTEL †

MAN MUSS DAS UNMÖGLICHE VERLANGEN, DAMIT DAS MÖGLICHE GELEISTET WIRD — H. v. MOLTKE

In dankbarer Würdigung ihres heldenhaften Einsatzes im Kampf für die Zukunft unseres Volkes verlieh der Führer dem Major Hartmann Grasser, Gruppenkommandeur in einem Jagdgeschwader, als 288. Soldaten, Oberleutnant Wolf Ettel, Staffelkapitän in einem Jagdgeschwader, als 289. Soldaten, Hauptmann Heinrich Prinz zu Sayn-Wittgenstein, Gruppenkommandeur in einem Nachtjagdgeschwader, als 290. Soldaten, und dem Oberleutnant Walter Nowotny, Staffelkapitän in einem Jagdgeschwader, als 293. Soldaten der deutschen Wehrmacht das

EICHENLAUB ZUM RITTERKREUZ DES EISERNEN KREUZES

Oberleutnant Ettel hat die Verleihung der hohen Auszeichnung nicht mehr erlebt. Er starb im Juli 1943 im Kampf gegen England den Heldentod

Oberleutnant NOWOTNY

WIE SIE DAS RITTERKREUZ ERWARBEN

Hauptmann LEHMANN — Hauptm. OBERLÄNDER — Oberleutnant ROEHRIG — Oberleutnant BÖWING-TREUDING †

Hauptmann Kurt Lehmann, Staffelkapitän in einem Kampfgeschwader, zeichnete sich besonders im letzten Winter bei den Kampf- und Versorgungseinsätzen in Cholm und Welikije Luki aus. Er hat über 80 Bahnhofsanlagen erfolgreich angegriffen, 17 Transportzüge und über 100 Fahrzeuge durch Volltreffer zerstört. — Hauptmann Oberländer, Flugzeugführer in einem Kampfgeschwader, tat sich besonders im Kampf um die Festung Stalingrad und durch zahlreiche Versorgungsflüge für eingeschlossene Heeresverbände hervor. — Oberleutnant Roehrig, Flugzeugführer in einem Jagdgeschwader, schoß 78 feindliche Flugzeuge ab. Von einem Feindflug an der Südfront kehrte er nicht zurück. — Oberleutnant Böwing-Treuding, Staffelführer in einem Jagdgeschwader, bezwang in zahlreichen Luftkämpfen 45 Feindflugzeuge, unter denen sich 20 Bomber und 15 Schlachtflugzeuge befanden. Der kühne Offizier starb den Heldentod. — Oberleutnant Franken, Flugzeugführer in einem Kampfgeschwader, gelang es, 46 000 BRT feindlichen Handelsschiffsraums zu versenken und weitere 56 000 BRT durch Torpedotreffer schwer zu beschädigen. — Oberfeldwebel Herbert Kaiser, in einem Jagdgeschwader, errang in zahlreichen harten Luftkämpfen 53 Luftsiege.

PK Aufn. Kriegsberichter Wanderer (Sch 1), Scherl-OKW (10)

Oberleutnant FRANKEN — Oberfeldwebel KAISER

Acknowledgement of the new bearer of the *Ritterkreuz* and *Eichenlaub* in the *Luftwaffe-Illustrierte* "Der Adler."

On September 8, 1943, five more enemy planes fell victim to Nowotny. With that another magic number is reached. The ground crew decorates his Focke-Wulf with an oak wreath and the number "200."

In remembrance, a picture of the successful three: the Fw 190, the pilot, and his loyal *1. Wart*.

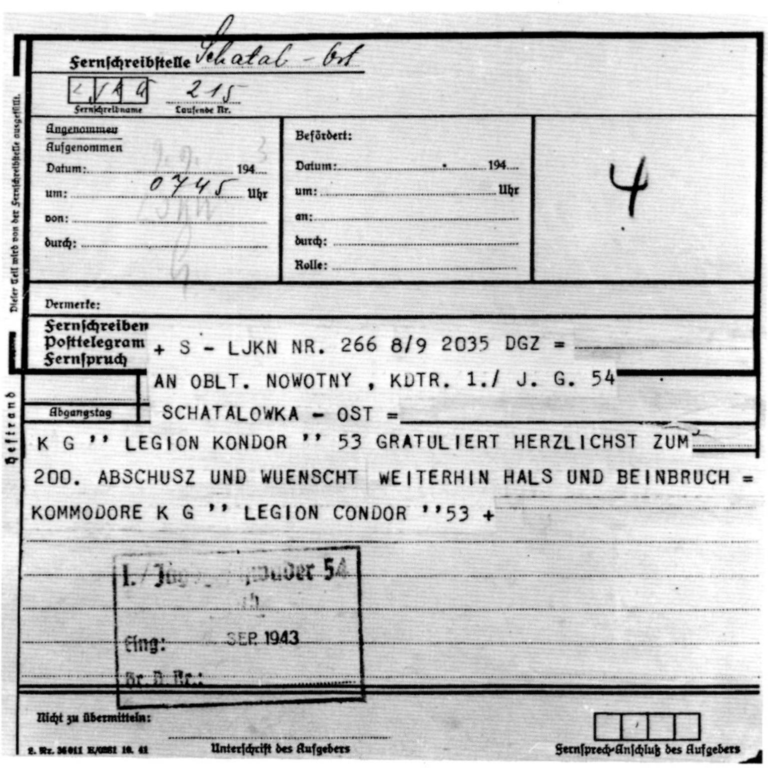

Fernschreibstelle Schatal-Ost

Fernschreibname / Laufende Nr. 215

Angenommen / Aufgenommen
Datum: 194..
um: 0745 Uhr
von:
durch:

Befördert:
Datum: 194..
um: Uhr
an:
durch:
Rolle:

4

Vermerke:

Fernschreiben / Posttelegram / Fernspruch + S - LJKN NR. 266 8/9 2035 DGZ =

AN OBLT. NOWOTNY , KDTR. 1./ J. G. 54

Abgangstag SCHATALOWKA - OST =

K G '' LEGION KONDOR '' 53 GRATULIERT HERZLICHST ZUM

200. ABSCHUSZ UND WUENSCHT WEITERHIN HALS UND BEINBRUCH =

KOMMODORE K G '' LEGION CONDOR ''53 +

I./Jagdgeschwader 54
Eing: SEP 1943
Br. B. Nr.:

Nicht zu übermitteln:

Unterschrift des Aufgebers

Fernsprech-Anschluß des Aufgebers

A congratulatory telegram from the *Kommodore* KG 53 "Legion Condor" for the 200th air victory.

Begleitschutz for the St.G. "Immelmann" No. 2. The *Stukas* fulfill their task. The *Jagdschutz* flies around once more, and the unit gives notice of their departure.

On September 15, 1943, Nowotny shoots down five more enemy planes in the Schatalowka area, and with that wings his 215th air victory. *Oberstlt.* Pressler is again one of the first well wishers. Nowotny shows him the "Abschuflhose," and says: "These pants have accompanied me since my first mission, on which I shot down three Bolsheviks, and then when I was hit myself near Ösel and had to paddle for three days in the waters of the Baltic Sea. Since then my 'Abschuflhose' are with me during every mission."

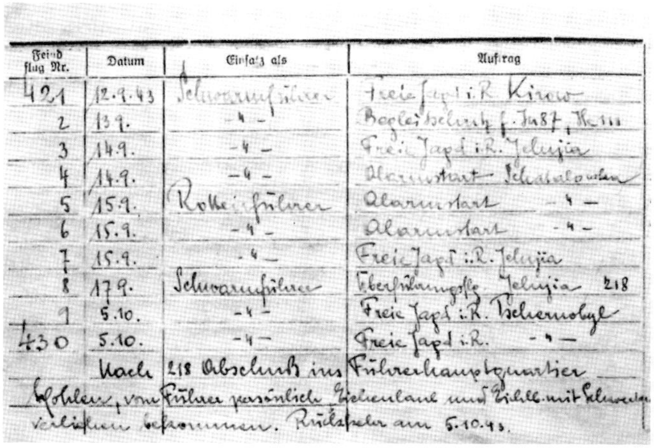

Feindflug Nr.	Datum	Einsatz als	Auftrag
421	12.9.43	Schwarmführer	Freie Jagd i.R. Kirow
2	13.9.	-"-	Begleitschutz f. Ju87, He111
3	14.9.	-"-	Freie Jagd i.R. Jelnja
4	14.9.	-"-	Alarmstart [illegible]
5	15.9.	Rottenführer	Alarmstart -"-
6	15.9.	-"-	Alarmstart -"-
7	15.9.	-"-	Freie Jagd i.R. Jelnja
8	17.9.	Schwarmführer	Überführungsflg. Jelnja 218
9	5.10.	-"-	Freie Jagd i.R. [illegible]
430	5.10.	-"-	Freie Jagd i.R. -"-

Nach 218 Abschuß ins Führerhauptquartier [illegible], vom Führer persönlich Eichenlaub und [illegible] mit Schwertern verliehen bekommen. Rückfahrt am 5.10.43.

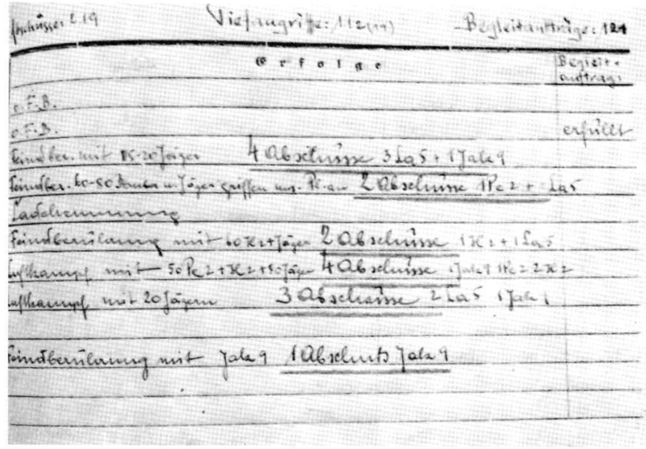

[illegible] 219 Tiefangriffe: 112 (14) Begleitaufträge: 124

Erfolge	Begleitaufträge
o.F.B.	
o.F.B.	erfüllt
Feindber. mit 15-20 Jägern 4 Abschüsse 3 La 5 + 1 Jak 9	
Feindber. 60-80 [illegible] u. Jäger [illegible] 2 Abschüsse 1 Pe 2 + [illegible] La 5	
[illegible]	
Feindberührung mit 60 [illegible] + Jäger 2 Abschüsse 1 [illegible] + 1 La 5	
Luftkampf mit 50 Pe 2 + [illegible] + 50 Jäger 4 Abschüsse 1 Jak 9 1 Pe 2 2 [illegible]	
Luftkampf mit 20 Jägern 3 Abschüsse 2 La 5 1 Jak 9	
Feindberührung mit Jak 9 1 Abschuß Jak 9	

Two La 5s and a Jak 9 fall victim to his aircraft weapons on September 9, 1943: 216-218th air victory. *Hauptmann* Walter Nowotny is ordered to headquarters, and is well due for the *Eichenlaub mit Schwerten*.

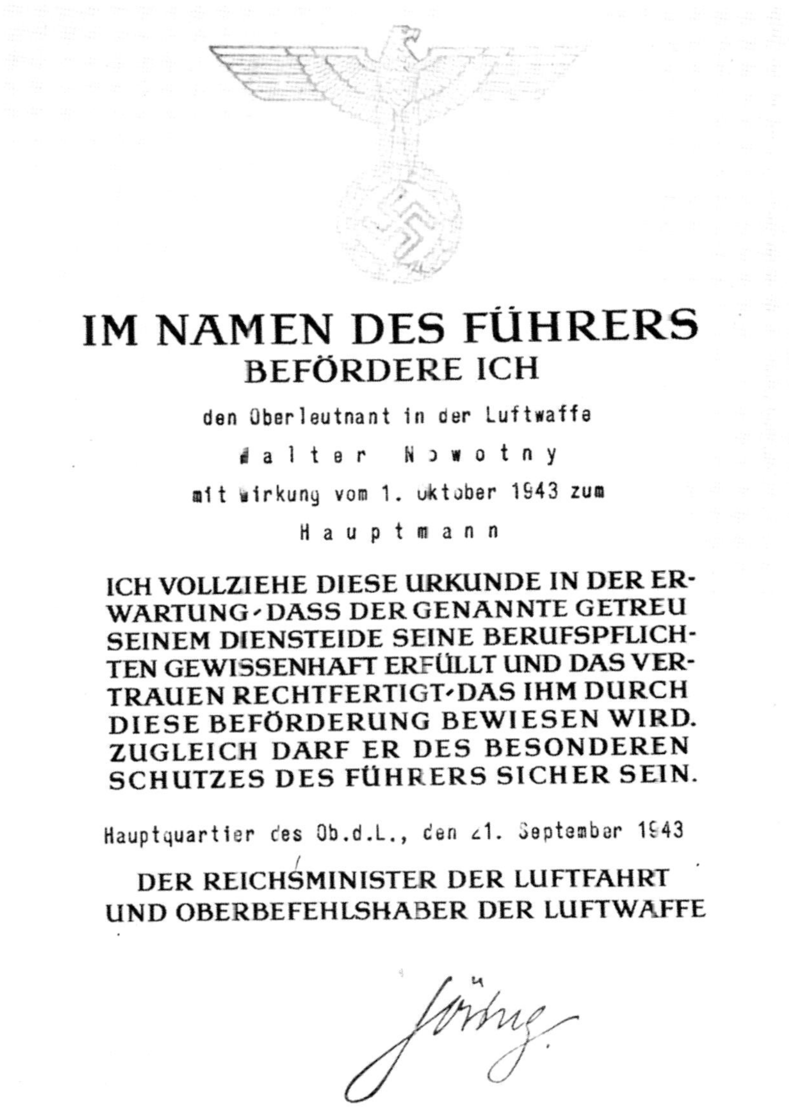

IM NAMEN DES FÜHRERS
BEFÖRDERE ICH

den Oberleutnant in der Luftwaffe

W a l t e r   N o w o t n y

mit Wirkung vom 1. Oktober 1943 zum

H a u p t m a n n

ICH VOLLZIEHE DIESE URKUNDE IN DER ERWARTUNG, DASS DER GENANNTE GETREU SEINEM DIENSTEIDE SEINE BERUFSPFLICHTEN GEWISSENHAFT ERFÜLLT UND DAS VERTRAUEN RECHTFERTIGT, DAS IHM DURCH DIESE BEFÖRDERUNG BEWIESEN WIRD. ZUGLEICH DARF ER DES BESONDEREN SCHUTZES DES FÜHRERS SICHER SEIN.

Hauptquartier des Ob.d.L., den 21. September 1943

DER REICHSMINISTER DER LUFTFAHRT UND OBERBEFEHLSHABER DER LUFTWAFFE

Göring

As of October 1, 1943, Walter Nowotny is promoted to *Hauptmann*. With this his military dedication is openly recognized.

On September 22, 1943, *Hauptmann* Nowotny receives the *Eichenlaub* and the *Eichenlaub mit Schwerten zum Ritterkreuz* from Adolf Hitler. He is the 37th soldier of the German *Wehrmacht* who has received this high honor. With Walter Nowotny they receive their decoration, from the left: Major Hartmann Grasser (EL), *Hauptmann* Heinrich Prinz zu Sayn-Wittgenstein (EL), and *Hauptmann* Günther Rall (Schw.).

IM NAMEN
DES DEUTSCHEN VOLKES
VERLEIHE ICH
DEM HAUPTMANN
WALTER NOWOTNY
DAS EICHENLAUB MIT SCHWERTERN
ZUM RITTERKREUZ
DES EISERNEN KREUZES

FÜHRERHAUPTQUARTIER
DEN 22. SEPTEMBER 1943

DER FÜHRER
UND OBERSTE BEFEHLSHABER
DER WEHRMACHT

The valuable conferment certificate. With 218 air victories *Hauptmann* Nowotny sets himself at the top of all German fighter pilots. *Major* Hans Philipp follows with 203, and *Major* Hermann Graf with 202 air victories. *Hauptmann* Günther Rall reached the magic number "200," as well.

After the conferment of the *Schwerter* an extended leave should follow, but Nowotny knows how much he is needed in his *Geschwader* on the Front. He returns back prematurely to his *Gruppe* on October 5, 1943. The face of the *Kommodore* (picture) shows joy as well as amazement.

Nowotny's beaming laughter is proof that he feels his best with his comrades. The picture is taken in front of one of his oldest planes, Hans Clausen's "Weifle 9."

The month of October 1943 brings glorious Autumn weather. The Soviets are pushing against German positions and much is going on in the skies over Russia. *Hauptmann* Nowotny is running with his men on a mission. The number of air victories speak for themselves:

10/5	No. 219	1 Jak 9
10/7	No. 220-223	3 Airacobra, 1 P 40
10/9	No. 224-231	6 Airacobra, IL 2 (3 missions)
10/11	No. 232-235	2 P 40, 1 Airacobra, 1 Lagg 3
10/12	No. 236-238	3 Lagg 3
10/13	No. 239-244	4 La 5, 1 Lagg 3, 1 IL 2
10/14	No. 245-257	2 P 40, 2 Lagg 3, 2 La 5

This picture was taken on October 13, 1943. Six air victories in one day. The exhausted facial expression of the young *Hauptmann* says everything.

The following four pictures show how well the tension eases after hard air combat. First a cigarette, then Nowotny reports to his comrades.

The *Kommodore* Hubertus v. Bonin has also arrived and reports. On the back of the top picture Nowotny writes, "Quax always talks." Slowly his relieved laugh returns. The true "Katschmarek" Schnörrer defeated his 28th opponent during these days.

In a ten-minute difficult air battle *Hptm.* Nowotny shoots down a P 40 in the Karatschew area on October 14, 1943. The 250th enemy has fallen. The planes returning home are greeted with fireworks from the signal ammunition from the flak area. Cheers and joy are among the comrades, and the head of a champagne bottle is broken on a fighter plane. In the following night Nowotny wants to really relax for once. With the staff doctor he flies to Wilna in a Me 108 "Taifun." In the "Ria" bar a phone call from the *Führer's* headquarters in East Prussia reaches him. Hitler congratulates him for receiving the *Brillant*. Nowotny is ordered to Rastenburg on October 19, 1943.

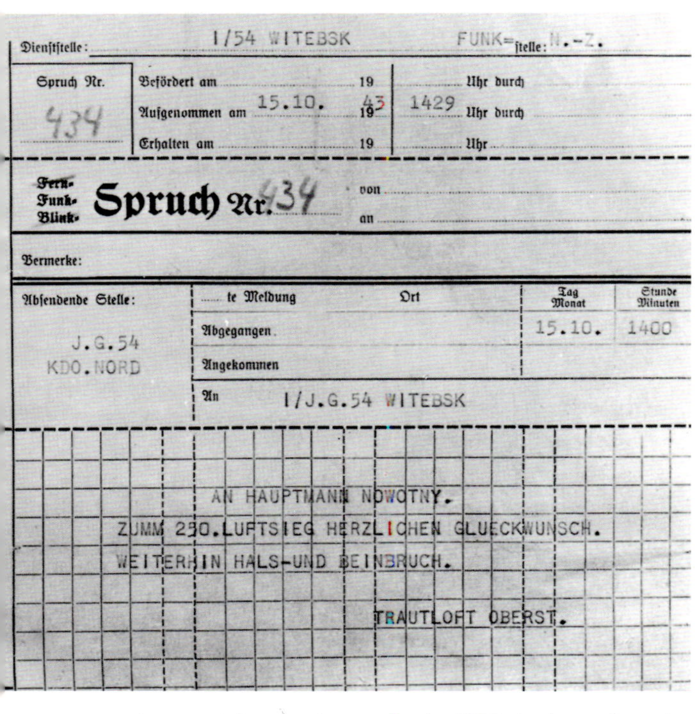

Dienststelle: I/54 WITEBSK FUNK-stelle: N.-Z.

Spruch Nr. 434 — Befördert am ... 19 ... Uhr durch — Aufgenommen am 15.10. 1943 1429 Uhr durch — Erhalten am ... 19 ... Uhr

Fern- Funk- Blink- Spruch Nr. 434 von ... an ...

Vermerke:

Absendende Stelle:	...te Meldung	Ort	Tag Monat	Stunde Minuten
J.G.54 KDO.NORD	Abgegangen		15.10.	1400
	Angekommen			
	An I/J.G.54 WITEBSK			

AN HAUPTMANN NOWOTNY.
ZUMM 250.LUFTSIEG HERZLICHEN GLUECKWUNSCH.
WEITERHIN HALS-UND BEINBRUCH.
TRAUTLOFT OBERST.

A congratulatory telegram for the 250th air victory from the former *Kommodore* of JG 54, Hannes Trautloft.

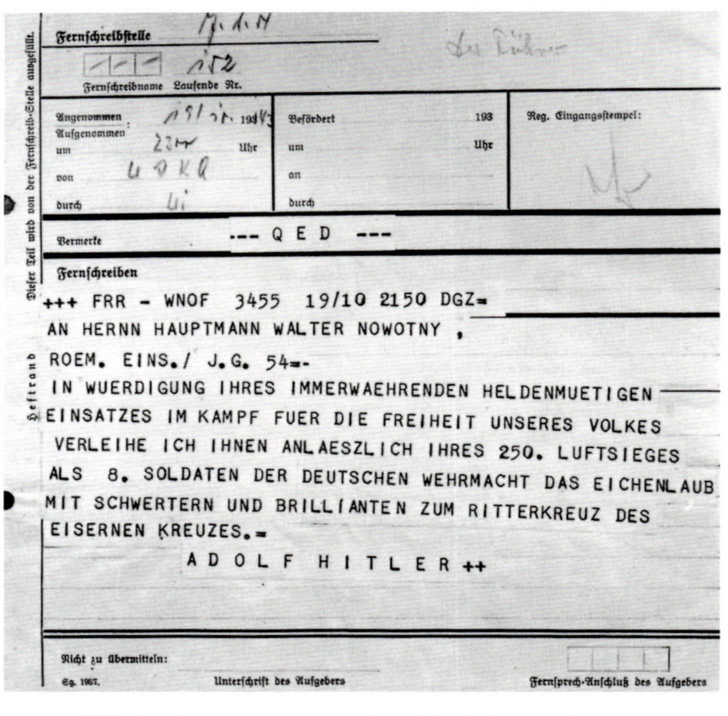

Dieser Teil wird von der Fernschreib-Stelle ausgefüllt.

Fernschreibstelle — Fernschreibname Laufende Nr. 152

Angenommen / Aufgenommen um 2314 Uhr von ... durch ... — Befördert ... 193 ... um ... Uhr an ... durch ... — Reg. Eingangsstempel:

Vermerke --- Q E D ---

Fernschreiben

+++ FRR - WNOF 3455 19/10 2150 DGZ=
AN HERNN HAUPTMANN WALTER NOWOTNY ,
ROEM. EINS./ J.G. 54=-
IN WUERDIGUNG IHRES IMMERWAEHRENDEN HELDENMUETIGEN
EINSATZES IM KAMPF FUER DIE FREIHEIT UNSERES VOLKES
VERLEIHE ICH IHNEN ANLAESZLICH IHRES 250. LUFTSIEGES
ALS 8. SOLDATEN DER DEUTSCHEN WEHRMACHT DAS EICHENLAUB
MIT SCHWERTERN UND BRILLIANTEN ZUM RITTERKREUZ DES
EISERNEN KREUZES.=
A D O L F H I T L E R ++

Heftrand

Nicht zu übermitteln: — Unterschrift des Aufgebers — Fernsprech-Anschluß des Aufgebers

Hitler's telegram on the occasion of the *Brillant* conferment.

Before departure to East Prussia. Left Schnörrer. In the background is General Ritter von Greim's He 111.

Frontnachrichtenblatt der Luftwaffe Nr. 55

Träger des Eichenlaubes mit Schwertern und Brillanten zum Ritterkreuz des Eisernen Kreuzes

Hauptmann Walter Nowotny

Am 4. 9. 1942
Ritterkreuz des Eisernen Kreuzes

Am 9. 9. 1943
Eichenlaub zum Ritterkreuz des Eisernen Kreuzes

Am 22. 9. 1943
Eichenlaub mit Schwertern zum Ritterkreuz des Eisernen Kreuzes

Am 19. 10. 1943
Eichenlaub mit Schwertern und Brillanten zum Ritterkreuz des Eisernen Kreuzes

Der Oberbefehlshaber der Luftwaffe, Reichsmarschall Göring, richtete anläßlich der Verleihung des Eichenlaubes mit Schwertern und Brillanten zum Ritterkreuz des Eisernen Kreuzes am 20. 10. 1943 an Hauptmann Nowotny folgendes Glückwunschschreiben:

Lieber Nowotny! Sie haben in einem Siegeslauf ohnegleichen Kampferfolge errungen wie kein Jagdflieger vor Ihnen. Mit der Verleihung der Brillanten zum Eichenlaub mit Schwertern zum Ritterkreuz des Eisernen Kreuzes hat Ihr heldenhafter Einsatz in vielen hundert Luftkämpfen höchste Anerkennung durch den Führer gefunden. Voll Stolz beglückwünsche ich Sie, mein junger Kamerad, zu dieser nur den Tapfersten der Tapferen bestimmten Auszeichnung. Mit meiner Luftwaffe sieht in Ihnen das ganze deutsche Volk das strahlende Beispiel fanatischen Siegeswillens.

The Front newspaper of *Luftwaffe* No. 55 with *Reichsmarschall* Göring's good wishes.

On October 19, 1943, Walter Nowotny receives the *Eichenlaub mit Schwertern und Brillanten zum Ritterkreuz des Eisernen Kreuzes* from Hitler.

Hptm. Nowotny leaves the *Führer's* headquarters in Rastenburg. He is excited about the upcoming vacation in Vienna, and there is to be fun for all.

The parents are glad to have their youngest at home again for a few days.

With the parents for an evening at an operetta in casual society. In the foreground middle the composer of the operetta melodies, Heinrich Strecker.

His days on leave go by quickly like a flight. Relaxation is out of the question. The city of Vienna is celebrating their bearer of the *Brillant*. On Schönererstrafle 32 it is like Piccadilly Circus—reporters, well wishers, and many who ask for an autograph.

At his departure the Viennese population celebrates wildly once more. Nowotny walks through tightly packed rows of people to the vehicle that takes him to the airport.

Heartfelt farewell from his parents at the Wien-Schwechat airport. These pictures document the close relationship between parents and son.

In the cockpit of a He 111 the *Hauptmann* flies back to the Front. A last laugh and wink, then the long flight eastward. Walter Nowotny can finally rest, and he cannot keep his eyes open. This shot was not shown to the public. The reason: heroes should not be portrayed sleeping.

Beaming faces on the comrades in the unit. The *Gruppenarzt*, Dr. Vossber, and *Oblt*. Hübner, war correspondent, greet and congratulate Hauptmann *Nowotny* (picture above). Handshakes also on the runway. His comrades are excited about the return of their "Nowi." In the middle background is Rademacher.

Oberfeldwebel Otto Kittel is awarded with the *Ritterkreuz* on October 29, 1943, after 123 air victories. In the presence of the *Kommodore*, Major v. Bonin, *Oberst* Reufl places the medal around the neck of the successful fighter pilot.

Accompanied by *Gruppenkommandeurs Hptm.* Nowotny and *Oberst* Reufl, *Ofw.* Kittel inspects the *Gruppe*. In a small circle they are celebrating with coffee and cake. Far left *Hptm.* Nowotny, in the middle Otto Kittel, and far right the *Kommodore* JG 54.

After the *Brillant* conferment *Hptm.* Nowotny continues to lead his *Gruppe*. The feared grounding order in Rastenburg remains unspoken, and so he continues to fly against the enemy. Here with Schnörrer in front of a map in the combat post he is discussing a mission. Nowotny helps his friend with missions by taking over the function of the "Katschmarek." From then on "Quax" flies in a swerving motion over the area.

On the way to their quarters Karl Schnörrer describes how he instructed the Russian IL 2 "Stormovik" *Schlachtflugzeuge* (picture below). On the backside of the left picture is a comment written by Nowotny: "The quickest Rotte. Quax always talks."

In November 1943 fate hits hard twice. On the 11th Döbele collides in the air with a comrade in Witebsk on the border area and fatally crashes.

In a hangar the coffin is laid out with the mortal remains of a friend. *Hptm.* Nowotny, deeply moved, says goodbye to "his Toni."

Above: During the funeral service four successful comrades are on sentry duty. Front left: *Ofw.* Kittel, behind him *Ofw.* Rademacher. Right: *Ofw.* Wöhnert and *Ofw.* Tegtmeier (in the back).

Left: The *Kommodore*, *Major* v. Bonin, speaks a few words to honor the brave pilot.

Below: This picture of the *Kommandeur* is taken during these difficult days.

But life goes on. Man can allow himself many things, but not resignation. The annoying paper warfare claims many hours of the 22 year old *Kommandeur*. A light-hearted joke from "Quax" or the description of difficult air combat brings life to the "Bude" again.

On 12 November another stroke of fate hits the *Gruppe*. *Hauptmann* Nowotny and his "Katschmarek" find themselves in the Newel area in air combat with six Russian opponents. Nowotny shoots down the first one, as another one takes after him, but "Quax" is on his guard. Burning, this opponent crashes to the marshy ground. Suddenly Nowotny roars, "Quax, rip your plane to the left! You're on fire!" and soon thereafter: "Bale out, you can't land in the forests." Schnörrer tries to pull up his Focke-Wulf, but in vain. From an altitude of 70 m he jumps. The reserve shoot pulls out the main chute, but cannot slow down his fall. He hits down hard. Infantrymen rescue the badly injured man from the main lines. With a *Fieseler* "Storch" he is picked up, and Nowotny brings his friend into the *Luftwaffe* hospital Halle-Dölau with a Ju 52. Before the departure *Kommodore* v. Bonin reports.

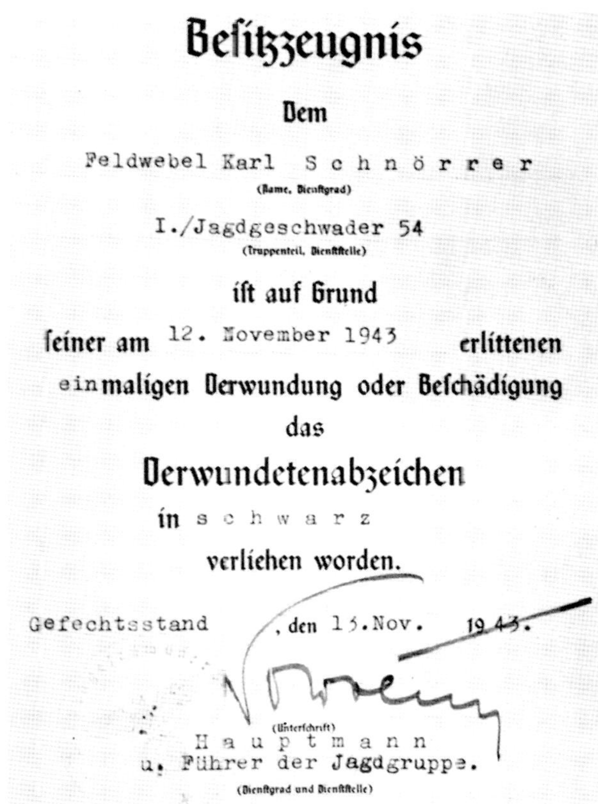

Besitzzeugnis

Dem

Feldwebel Karl Schnörrer
(Name, Dienstgrad)

I./Jagdgeschwader 54
(Truppenteil, Dienststelle)

ist auf Grund

seiner am 12. November 1943 erlittenen

einmaligen Verwundung oder Beschädigung

das

Verwundetenabzeichen

in schwarz

verliehen worden.

Gefechtsstand, den 13.Nov. 1943.

(Unterschrift)
Hauptmann
u. Führer der Jagdgruppe.
(Dienstgrad und Dienststelle)

The *Feldwebel* Karl Schnörrer receives the *Verwundetenabzeichen in Schwarz* for his injury.

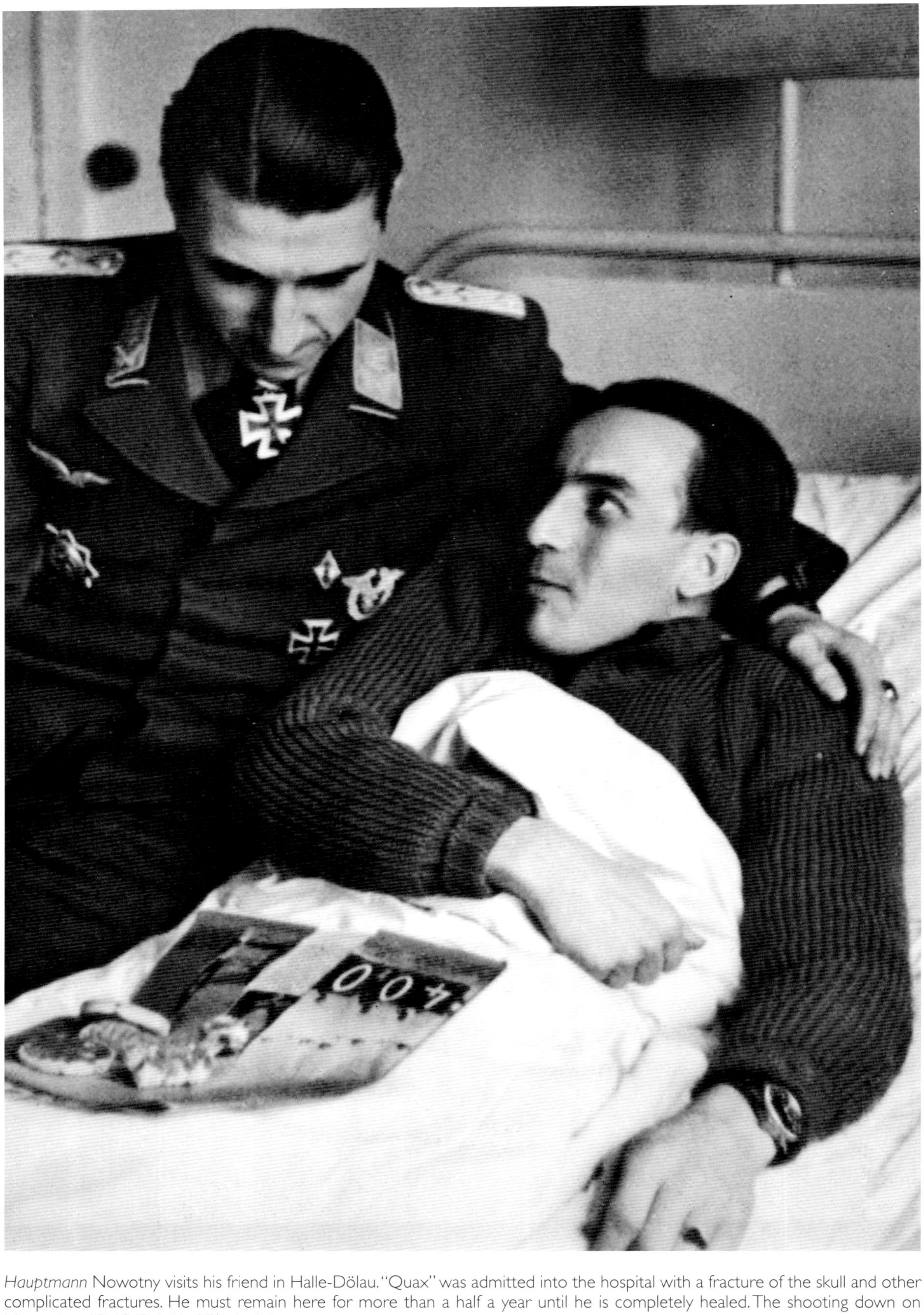

Hauptmann Nowotny visits his friend in Halle-Dölau. "Quax" was admitted into the hospital with a fracture of the skull and other complicated fractures. He must remain here for more than a half a year until he is completely healed. The shooting down on November 12, 1943, is his 37th air victory.

November brings Walter Nowotny the last missions and his last air victories on the Eastern Front. For Nowotny, as well as other bearers of the *Brillant* in the *Luftwaffe*, their time of active duty on the front comes to an end. Other uses are planned for him.

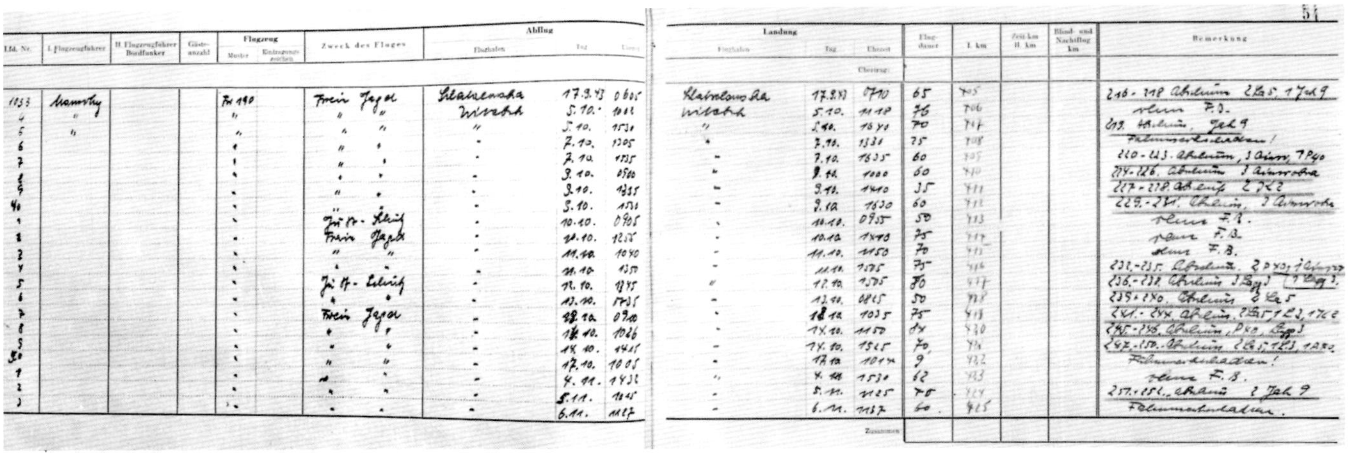

With *Uffz.* Ernst Richter as "Katschmarek," he takes off on November 15, 1943, for his last Front flight, and returns to the airfield in a swerving motion with two air victories: numbers 254 and 255. The last air victories on the Eastern Front. Walter Nowotny notes 255 confirmed and 50 unconfirmed air victories on the eastern *theater of war.*

On December 7, 1943—on Nowotny's 23rd birthday—the "Tag des deutschen Eisenbahnes" is being celebrated. During the celebration *Hauptmann* Nowotny presents the engineer Kindervater the *Ritterkreuz zum Kriegsverdienstkreuz*.

After the ceremony *Hauptmann* Nowotny is invited to coffee and cake by the management. The surprise was great, as a birthday cake with the number 23 is seen on the table.

Nowotny as the man who gives away the bride, and the witness to the marriage of his childhood friend, *Oblt.* Kurt Gindl, in Mistelback/NÖ.

Carefree days in the circle of friends in Kärnten. The third from the left—standing—Walter's bride.

Shortly before Christmas (on December 21, 1943), Nowotny visits the *Focke-Wulf-Werke*. With a Ju 86 E-2 he lands in Bad Eilsen. Prof. Tank receives his guest at his plane. Walter Nowotny forms friendships quickly with Prof. Kurt Tank and his Werkspiloten. The Fw 190 was exactly what he used when he achieved his great successes.

Group pictures with test pilots in front of an improved Fw 190. From the left: Hans Kampmeier, Werner Fink, Rolf Mondry, *Hptm.* Nowotny, and Alfred Motsch.

Hauptmann Nowotny, who now has a grounding order, does not miss out on an opportunity, and flies the fast Focke-Wulf in style.

Prof. Tank is the creator of not only fighter planes, but also many other types. Nowotny demonstrates the Fw 189, an *Aufklärer*, here.

The model of the Fw 190 that was given to him as a gift in memory of this visit is still today in the possession of the Nowotny family.

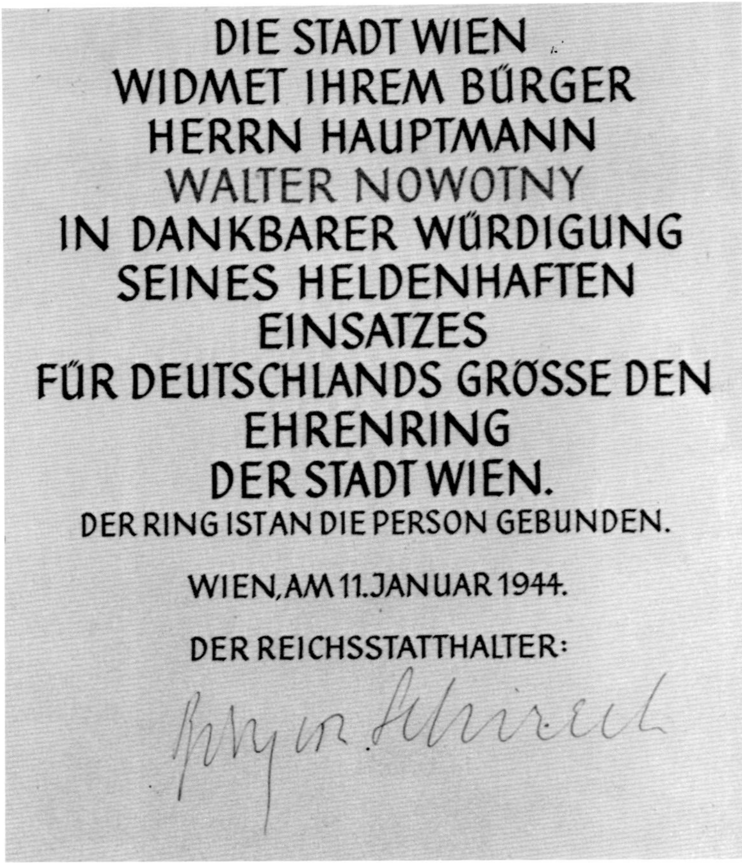

DIE STADT WIEN
WIDMET IHREM BÜRGER
HERRN HAUPTMANN
WALTER NOWOTNY
IN DANKBARER WÜRDIGUNG
SEINES HELDENHAFTEN
EINSATZES
FÜR DEUTSCHLANDS GRÖSSE DEN
EHRENRING
DER STADT WIEN.
DER RING IST AN DIE PERSON GEBUNDEN.

WIEN, AM 11. JANUAR 1944.

DER REICHSSTATTHALTER:

A special honor is given to *Hauptmann* Nowotny in January 1944. The city of Vienna awarded him with the *Ehrenring* of the city.

Geschwader JG 54 suffers a great loss on December 15, 1943: the *Kommodore*, *Oberstlt.* Hubertus v. Bonin, fell in air combat by Witebsk. He won 77 air victories, four of which were in Spain.

On January 18, 1944, the then *Oberbürgermeister* of Vienna, *Dipl.-Ing.* Blaschke, presents *Hauptmann* Nowotny with the city's *Ehrenring* during a small ceremony. The golden signet ring with Vienna's coat of arms is bound to the wearer; it was given back after Nowotny's death. Walter Nowotny always wore this ring proudly. Lower right: *General* Stümpfl congratulates *Hptm.* Nowotny for the conferment of the ring.

On January 20, 1944, a delegation of JG 54 visits the *Patenwerk* of the *Geschwader*, the office equipment factory in Zella-Mehlis, in Thüringen. The name Trautloft was then greatly associated with the *Geschwader*, even though *Oberst* Trautloft was active in the staff of the *General der Jagdflieger* (Galland).

Major Seiler also belongs with the guests of the company. From the left: Major Seiler, *Hauptmann* Nowotny, and *Hauptmann* Wübke.

Greeting of the guests in *Direktor* Anschütz's office.

Left above: *Hptm.* Nowotny during his visit at the company.

Middle right: A speech from *Direktor* Anschütz and *Hauptmann* Nowotny during a ceremony with company personnel.

The visit concludes with a get together.

Jagdfliegerschule Pau

In January 1944, *Hauptmann* Nowotny returns to his *Gruppe* on the Eastern Front for a few days. But already in February he is taken out of active duty by the *Führer*'s orders. He must say goodbye to his comrades of the *Gruppe* and the *Geschwader*. This is certainly not easy for Nowotny, because he owes his meteoric rise and success to his comrades.

During the beginning of April 1944 his parents receive the first letter from their son in Pau, Southern France. Walter Nowotny took over the management of *Jagdfliegerschule* I in Pau in order to impart his experience to the recruits. The top priority of the hour was: *Jagdflieger, Piloten, Jäger*!

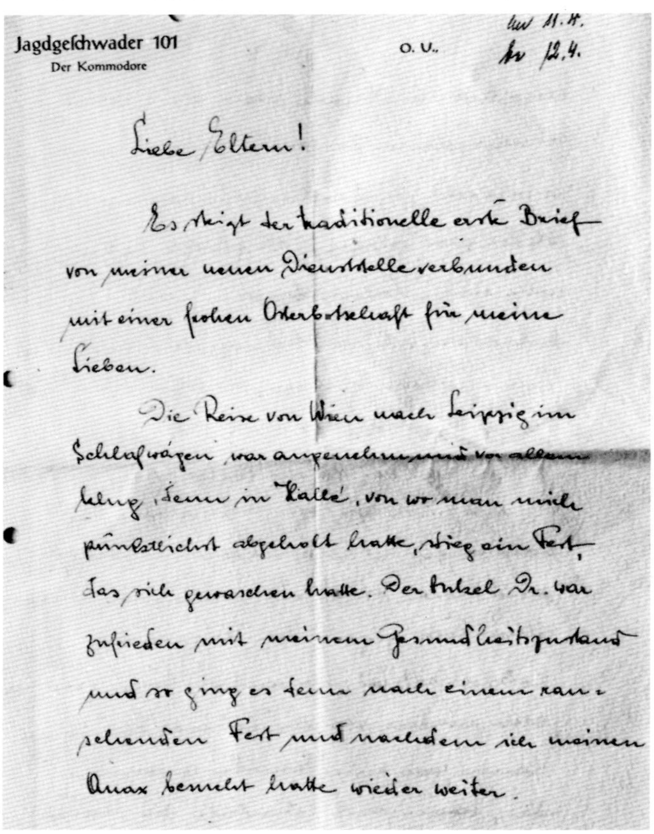

Jagdgeschwader 101
Der Kommodore
O. U., den 11.4. / den 12.4.

Liebe Eltern!

Es steigt der traditionelle erste Brief von meiner neuen Dienststelle verbunden mit einer frohen Osterbotschaft für meine Lieben.

Die Reise von Wien nach Leipzig im Schlafwagen war angenehm ~~und von allem~~ ... lung, denn in Halle, von wo man mich pünktlichst abgeholt hatte, stieg ein Fest, das sich gewaschen hatte. Der Onkel Dr. war zufrieden mit meinem Gesundheitszustand und so ging es denn nach einem rauschenden Fest und nachdem ich meinen Quax besucht hatte wieder weiter.

1

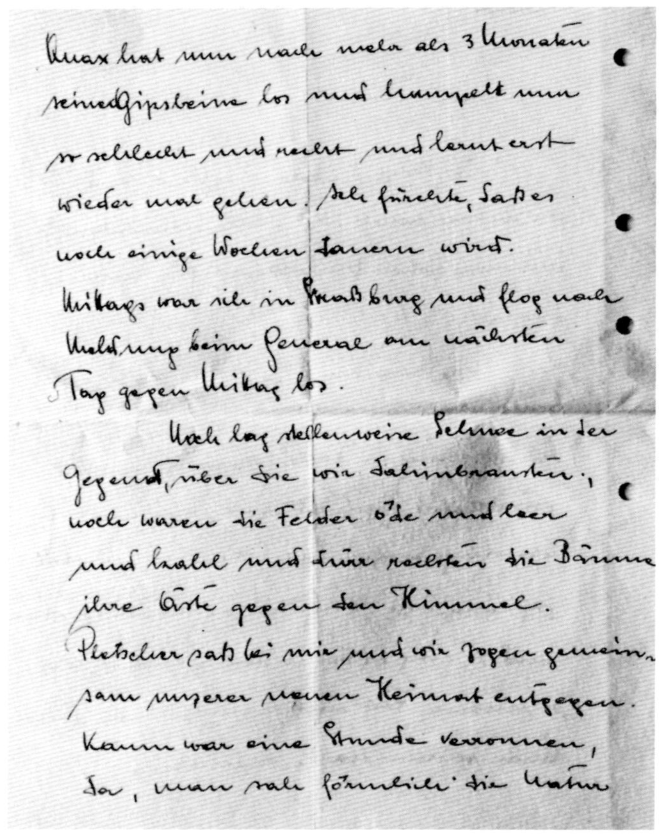

Quax hat nun nach mehr als 3 Monaten seine Gipsbeine los und trampelt nun so schlecht und recht und lernt erst wieder mal gehen. Ich fürchte, daß es noch einige Wochen dauern wird.

Mittags war ich in Straßburg und flog nach Meldung beim General am nächsten Tag gegen Mittag los.

Noch lag stellenweise Schnee in der Gegend, über die wir dahinbrausten, noch waren die Felder öde und leer und kahl und dürr reckten die Bäume ihre Äste gegen den Himmel. Pretscher saß bei mir und wir zogen gemeinsam unserer neuen Heimat entgegen. Kaum war eine Stunde verronnen, da, man sah förmlich die Natur

2

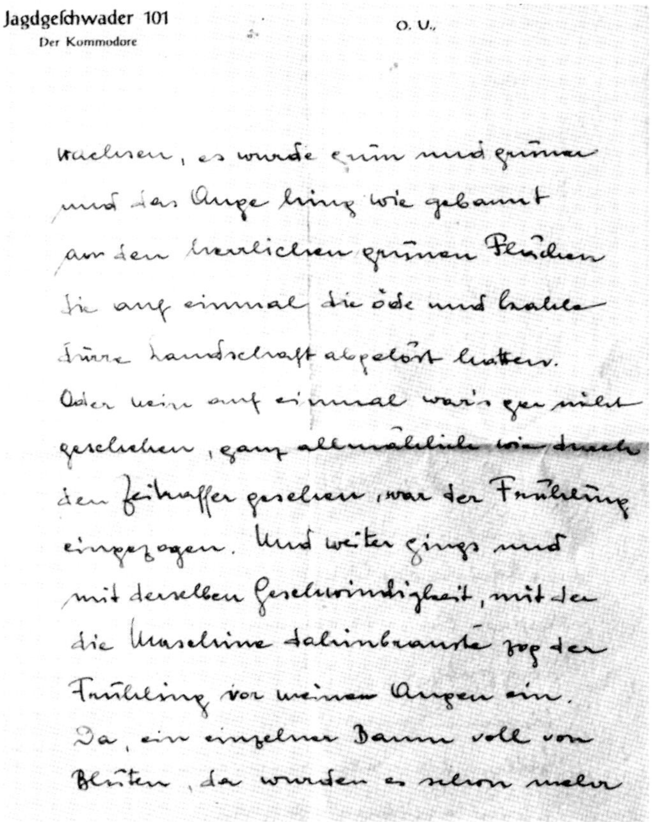

Jagdgeschwader 101
Der Kommodore
O. U.,

wachsen, es wurde grün und grüner und das Auge hing wie gebannt an den herrlichen grünen Flächen die auf einmal die öde und kahle dürre Landschaft abgelöst hatten. Oder nein auf einmal war's gar nicht geschehen, ganz allmählich wie durch den Zeitraffer gesehen, war der Frühling eingezogen. Und weiter gings und mit derselben Geschwindigkeit, mit der die Maschine dahinbrauste zog der Frühling vor meinen Augen ein. Da, ein einzelner Baum voll von Blüten, da wurden es schon mehr

3

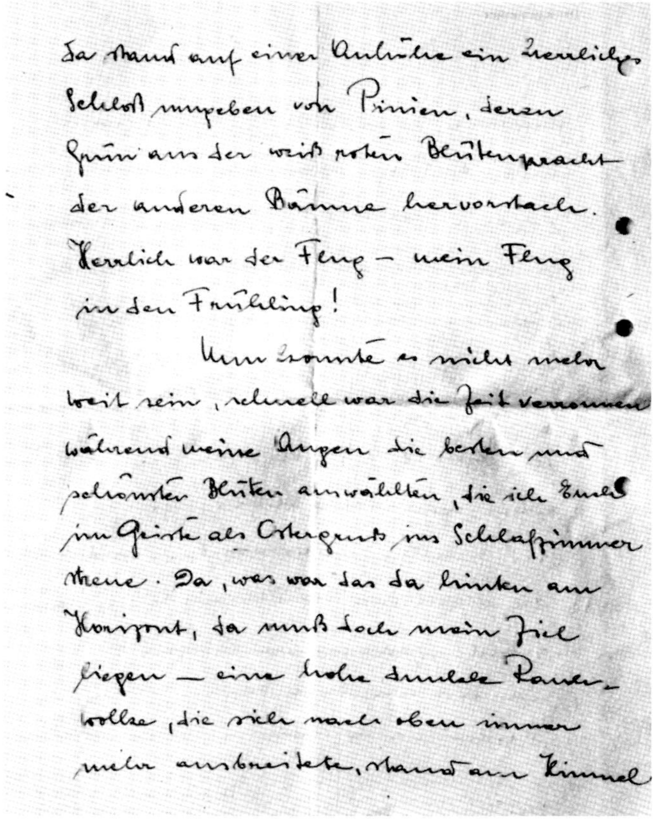

da stand auf einer Anhöhe ein herrliches Schloß umgeben von Pinien, deren Grün aus der weiß roten Blütenpracht der anderen Bäume hervorstach. Herrlich war der Flug – mein Flug in den Frühling!

Nun konnte es nicht mehr weit sein, schnell war die Zeit verronnen während meine Augen die besten und schönsten Blüten auswählten, die ich Euch im Geiste als Ostergruß ins Schlafzimmer stelle. Da, was war das da hinten am Horizont, da muß doch mein Ziel liegen – eine hohe dunkle Rauchwolke, die sich nach oben immer mehr ausbreitete, stand am Himmel

4

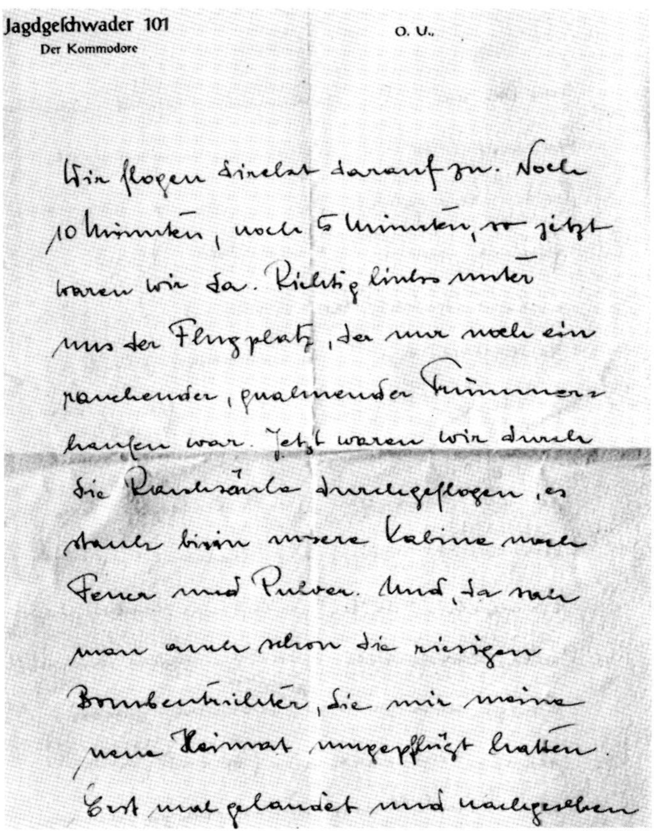

Jagdgeschwader 101
Der Kommodore
O. U.,

Wir flogen direkt darauf zu. Noch 10 Minuten, noch 5 Minuten, so jetzt waren wir da. Richtig links unter uns der Flugplatz, der nur noch ein rauchender, qualmender Trümmerhaufen war. Jetzt waren wir durch die Rauchsäule durchgeflogen, es stank bis in unsere Kabine nach Feuer und Pulver. Und, da sah man auch schon die riesigen Bombentrichter, die mir meine neue Heimat umgepflügt hatten. Erst mal gelandet und nachgesehen

5

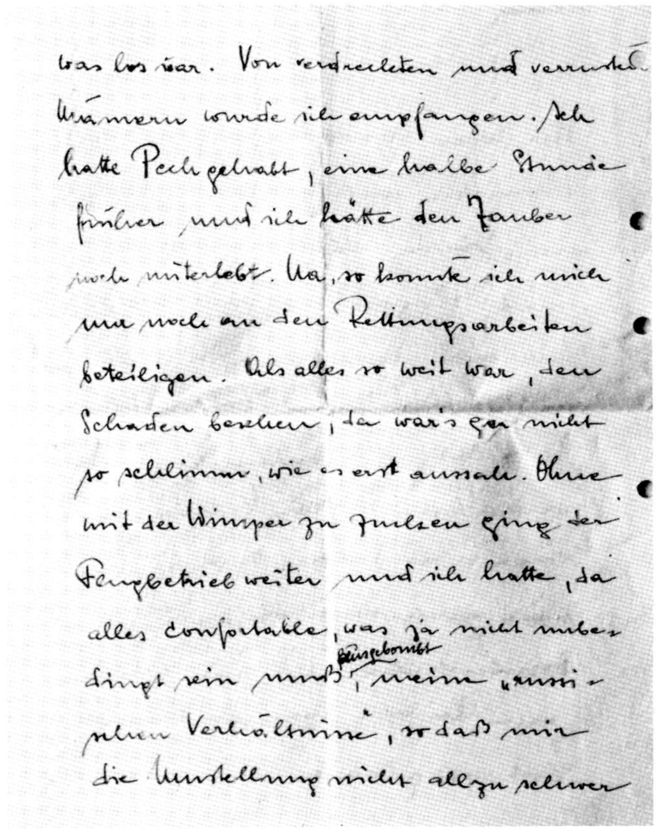

was los war. Von verdreckten und verrußten Männern wurde ich empfangen. Ich hatte Pech gehabt, eine halbe Stunde früher, und ich hätte den Zauber noch miterlebt. Na, so konnte ich mich nur noch an den Rettungsarbeiten beteiligen. Als alles so weit war, den Schaden besehen, da war's gar nicht so schlimm, wie es erst aussah. Ohne mit der Wimper zu zucken ging der Flugbetrieb weiter und ich hatte, da alles comfortable, was ja nicht unbedingt sein muß, ausgebombt, meine „russischen Verhältnisse", so daß mir die Umstellung nicht allzu schwer

6

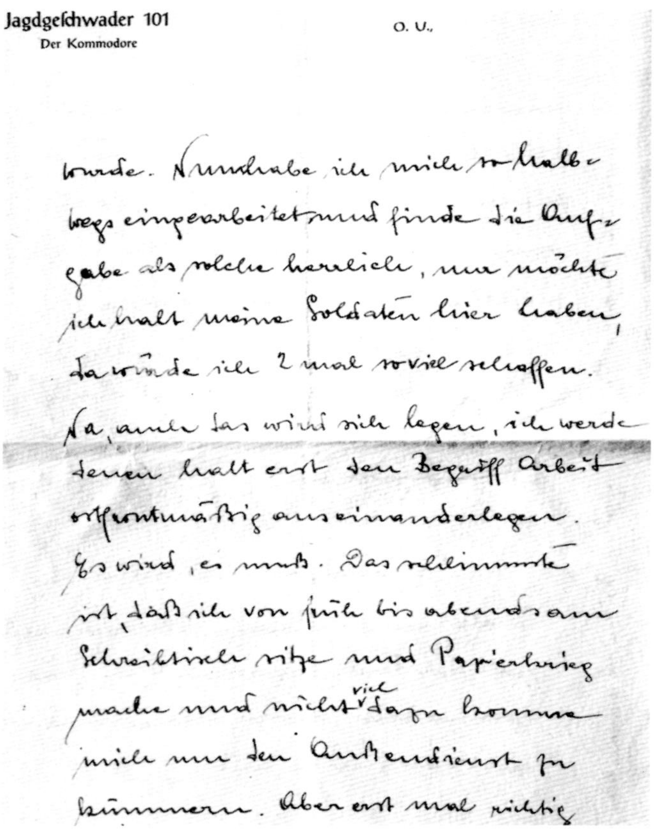

Jagdgeschwader 101
Der Kommodore

O. U.,

wurde. Nun habe ich mich so halb-
wegs eingearbeitet und finde die Auf-
gabe als solche herrlich, nur möchte
ich halt meine Soldaten hier haben,
da würde ich 2 mal soviel schaffen.
Na, auch das wird sich legen, ich werde
denen halt erst den Begriff Arbeit
[illegible] auseinanderlegen.
Es wird, es muß. Das schlimmste
ist daß ich von früh bis abends am
Schreibtisch sitze und Papierkrieg
mache und nicht viel dazu komme
mich um den Außendienst zu
kümmern. Aber erst mal richtig

7

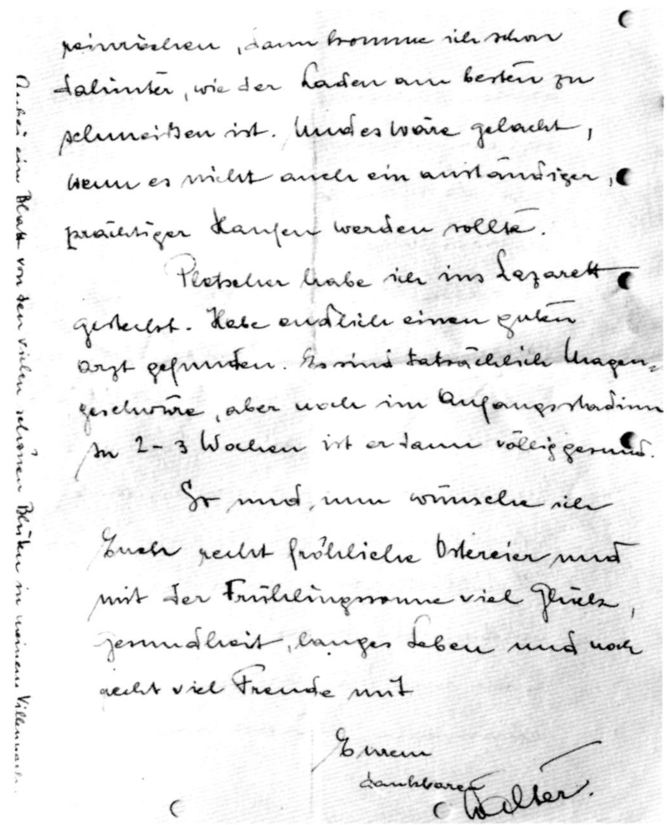

reinriechen, dann komme ich schon
dahinter, wie der Laden am besten zu
schmeißen ist. Und es wäre gelacht,
wenn es nicht auch ein anständiger,
prächtiger Haufen werden sollte.

Plötzlich habe ich ins Lazarett
gesteckt. Habe endlich einen guten
Arzt gefunden. Es sind tatsächlich Magen-
geschwüre, aber noch im Anfangsstadium
in 2-3 Wochen ist er dann völlig gesund.

So und, nun wünsche ich
Euch recht fröhliche Ostereier und
mit der Frühlingssonne viel Glück,
Gesundheit, langes Leben und noch
recht viel Freude mit

Euren
dankbaren
Walter.

Anbei ein Blatt von den vielen schönen Blättern in meinem Villenviert.

8

The flight to Pau that was so romantically described here takes place on March 27, 1944. A *Flügschüler* took this shot from the *Nordplatz*. In three waves, to each 24 "Liberators," the Americans fly over the *Südplatz*, and while two waves unload their bombs, the third flies to an unknown destination.

Nowotny attacks his new assignment with vigor. The presence alone of the young, successful *Kommodore* goads on the instructors and their budding pilots enormously. Everything goes like clockwork. This shot shows *Hptm.* Nowotny in front of the wing of a Focke-Wulf "Weihe" in Pau.

Flugschüler in front of a large number of Me 109G-12s, the two-seater "Gustavs." The light, unarmed *Vögel* were gladly flown by the flight instructors in aerobatics.

On 3 May Walter Nowotny has an experience that confirms the proverb of a small world. After many years, two former *Volksschule* comrades meet in Cuxac, a small city in Southern France: the bearer of the *Brillant*, *Hptm*. Walter Nowotny, and the *Unteroffizer* Franz Bruckner. Both are excited to see each other again, as is shown in the opposite pictures. In the officers' mess of the *Nachrichtereinheit* that Franz Bruckner belongs to a *Schrammelquartett* plays, and a typical Viennese atmosphere is soon reigning in the hall. An unforgettable experience for all who are present for this reunion.

On the *Süd* and *Nordplatz*, in Pau, air traffic is heavy. Advanced *Flugschüler* take off with the French Dewoitine 520 for target practice. The plane is armed with *Maschinengewehr*, which often jams. The young pilots gladly fly the Dewoitine 520.

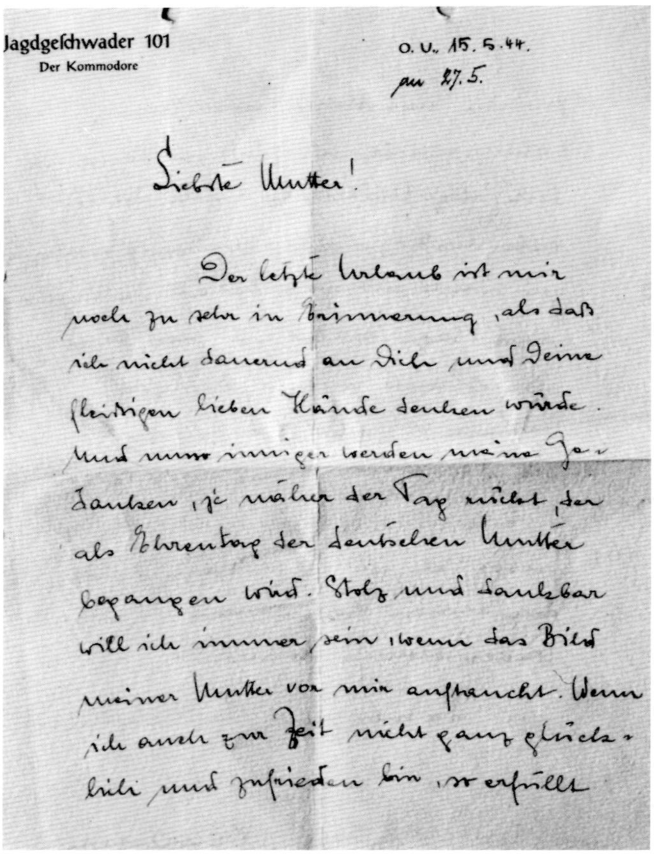

Jagdgeschwader 101
Der Kommodore

O. U., 15. 5. 44.
an 27.5.

Liebste Mutter!

Der letzte Urlaub ist mir noch zu sehr in Erinnerung, als daß ich nicht dauernd an Dich und Deine fleißigen lieben Hände denken würde. Und umso inniger werden meine Gedanken, je näher der Tag rückt, der als Ehrentag der deutschen Mutter begangen wird. Stolz und dankbar will ich immer sein, wenn das Bild meiner Mutter vor mir auftaucht. Wenn ich auch zur Zeit nicht ganz glücklich und zufrieden bin, so erfüllt

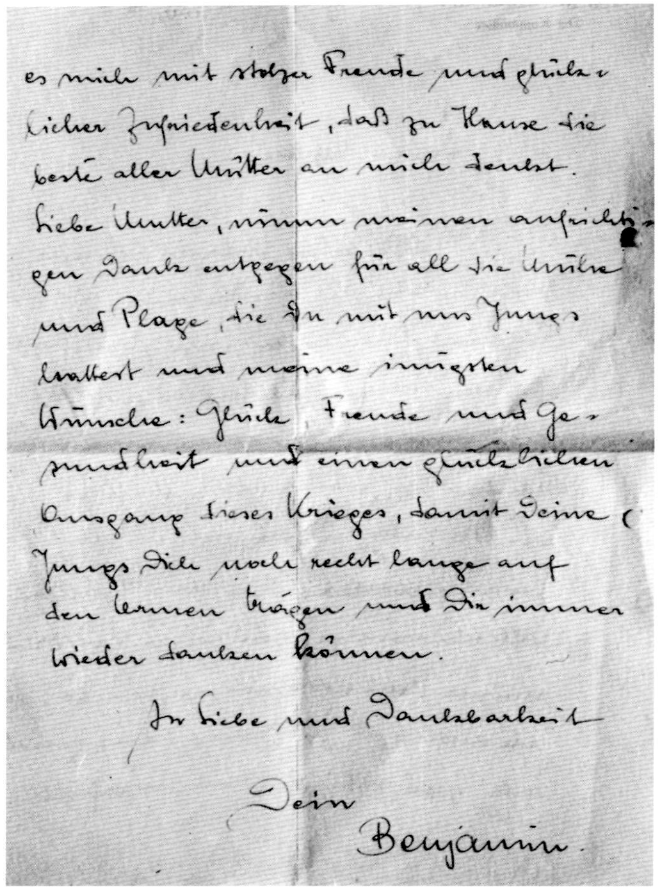

es mich mit stolzer Freude und glücklicher Zufriedenheit, daß zu Hause die beste aller Mütter an mich denkt. Liebe Mutter, nimm meinen aufrichtigen Dank entgegen für all die Mühe und Plage, die Du mit uns Jungs hattest und meine innigsten Wünsche: Glück, Freude und Gesundheit und einen glücklichen Ausgang dieses Krieges, damit Deine Jungs Dich noch recht lange auf den Armen tragen und Dir immer wieder danken können.

In Liebe und Dankbarkeit

Dein

Benjamin.

Letter to his mother on Mother's Day, May 15, 1944.

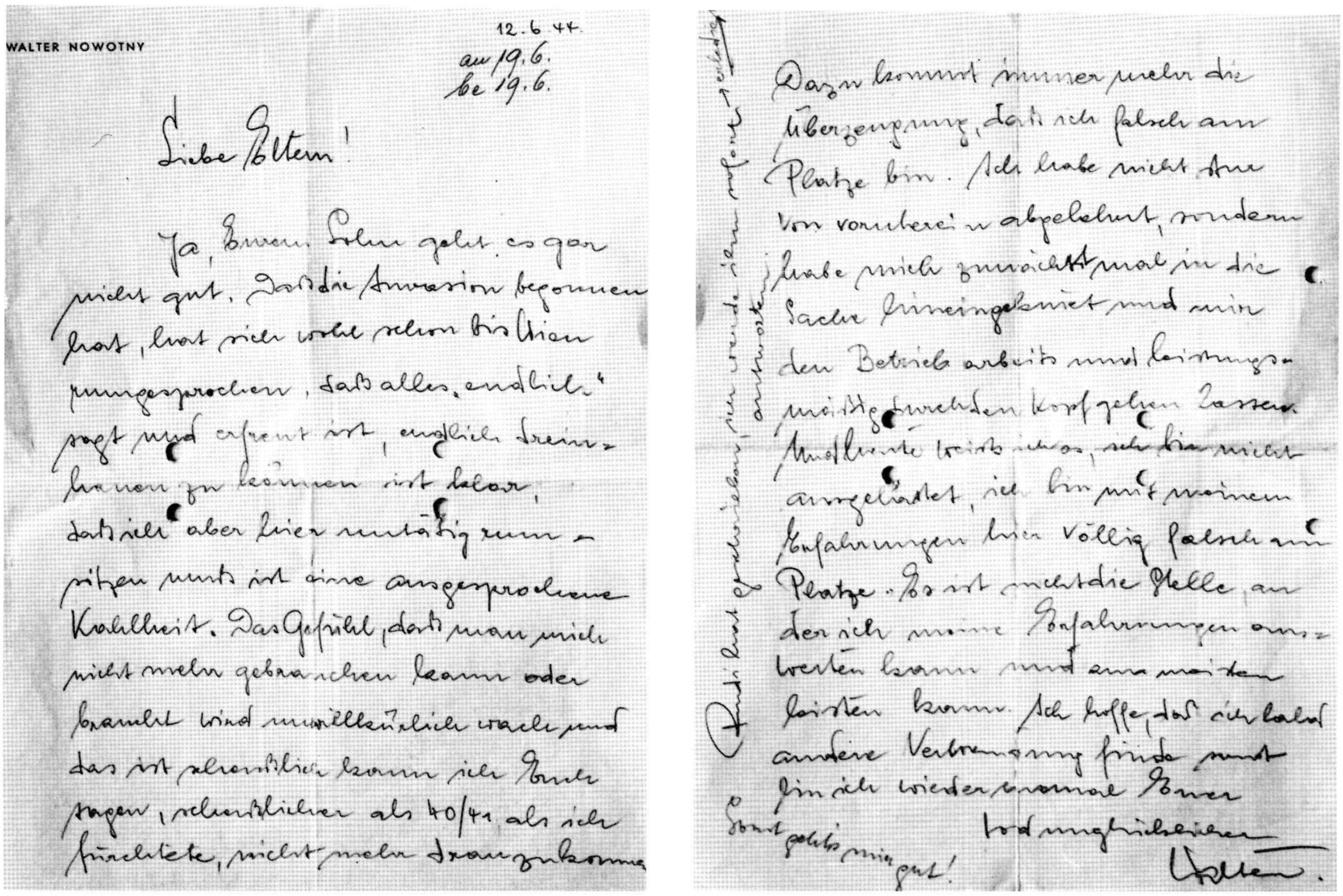
WALTER NOWOTNY

12.6.44.
an 19.6.
be 19.6.

Liebe Eltern!

Ja, Eurem Sohn geht es gar nicht gut. Daß die Invasion begonnen hat, hat sich wohl schon bis Wien herumgesprochen, daß alles „endlich" sagt und erfreut ist, endlich dreinhauen zu können ist klar, daß ich aber hier untätig herumsitzen muß ist eine ausgesprochene [illegible]. Das Gefühl, daß man mich nicht mehr gebrauchen kann oder braucht wird unwillkürlich wach und das ist schrecklich kann ich Euch sagen, schrecklicher als 40/41 als ich fürchtete, nicht mehr dranzukommen.

Dazu kommt immer mehr die Überzeugung, daß ich falsch am Platze bin. Ich habe nicht Arme von vornherein abgelehnt, sondern habe mich zunächst mal in die Sache hineingekniet und mir den Betrieb arbeits und leistungsmäßig durch den Kopf gehen lassen. Und heute weiß ich es, ich bin nicht ausgelastet, ich bin mit meinen Erfahrungen hier völlig falsch am Platze. Es ist nicht die Stelle an der ich meine Erfahrungen auswerten kann und am meisten leisten kann. Ich hoffe, daß ich bald andere Verwendung finde und bin ich wieder einmal Euer

todunglücklicher

Walter.

Sonst geht's mir gut!

Rudi hat geschrieben, ich werde ihm morgen antworten.

Letter to his parents on June 12, 1944.

Hauptmann Nowotny sets up a handball team during this time. He chooses excellent athletes from units of the *Luftwaffe*, and soon the team is successfully challenging strong opponents. These three shots are taken in August 1944 in Berlin. In a championship game, Nowotny's "Rote Adler" are up against the German champions of 1944, the *Polizei-Sportverein Berlin*.

Kommando Nowotny

After Allied invasions in the west, June 6, 1944, begins a terrible time for Walter Nowotny. He thinks that he is forgotten by the *Luftwaffenführung*. His present assignment, which he started with great enthusiasm, does not satisfy him anymore. During this time he writes a letter to a friend that contains the following:

"...I will go crazy soon. I have a lot to do here that is gradually eating away at my nerves. Yeah, Quax, you wouldn't believe it; what no one has done up to now, not even the worst enemy, my students do effortlessly." Later he continues, "...And when I've atoned for my sins here, I will pick you up, even if by force, and then we'll be flying again, even if we're put into splints. My head is clear and my heart is in the right place, what more does Nowi 1 and 2 need. Get well soon and Horrido!

Your old friend Nowi"

The situation in the sky became uncertain over Southern France, as well. *Jagdfliegerschule* I is transferred back to the *Reichsgebiet*. On September 1, 1944, Walter Nowotny is promoted to Major. On 9 September he gives *Schulgeschwader* 101 and *Jagdfliegerschule* I over to the *Kommando*. Since July 1944 a few Me 262-*Turbinenjäger* take off from Lechfeld for their first, secret missions under *Hauptmann* Thierfelder. The *Kommando* proves itself, especially against the Americans' high flying *Aufklärer*. On July 7, 1944, Werner Thierfelder fatally crashes, and *Hauptmann* Horst Geyer—until now *Erprobungskommando* 25—takes over "*Kommando* 262 Lechfeld."

Major Nowotny is then retrained on the Me 110 in Landsberg, and the first Me 262 takeoffs in Lechfeld follow shortly thereafter. *Hauptmann* Geyer is annoyed with the *Flugschüler* Major Nowotny because he refuses the introductory flights on the Me 262 two-seater. Despite that, everything goes well.

On September 26, 1944, Major Nowotny is put in charge of the deployment of the first official *Düsenjäger-Jagdkommandos* Me 262, that customarily bear his name in the *Luftwaffe*: "Kommando Nowotny."

The flying personnel of "*Kommando* Nowotny" consist of experienced pilots of *Erpr.Kdo.* 262 Lechfeld (Geyer) in the first line. Experienced pilots from various *Jagdgeschwader*, that were just retrained on Me 262s, add to this. The ground crew contributes to 7. *Staffel* of the ZG 26.

At the end of September the *Kommando* reaches its group, and is transferred during the first days of October with 23 "Turbos" to the Achmer and Hesepe bei Osnabrück airports. On October 4, 1944, Nowotny's old friend, *Hauptmann* Alfred Teumer, was killed in an accident while turning into a landing. After the failure of the engine, Teumer tried to land in Hesepe. *Hauptmann* Eder, who also joined "Kommando Nowotny," had the difficult task of burying their comrade. Both places (Achmer and Hesepe) are supplied with a concrete runway, which is long enough to make the takeoff and landing of the Me 262 possible. A few days after the arrival of the *Kommando* it appears that the new garrison is unfavorably situated. In the main approaching corridor of the allied *Bomber* and *Jägerverbände* unpleasant surprises had to be reckoned with.

Typical characteristics of the "*Kommando* Nowotny" planes are the lightly speckled fins and yellow painted turbine rings. The fuselage and wings are speckled greenish-gray. Nowotny's "Turbo," "Weifle 1," bears the "grünes Herz" underneath the cabin and the signature "Nowi." These shots of the *Kommando* in parade formation were taken during a bad period of weather. In late autumn 1944 this would have not otherwise been possible.

After a long stay in a military hospital in Dölau, his severe injuries are healed enough so that Quax can finally return to flying. Retraining on the Me 262 is not considered, so he is transferred directly to Achmer to "his Nowi." On 16 October Major Nowotny presents his friend this replacement ID. His old ID was lost.

geb. am 22.3.19 in Nürnberg
(Ort, Kreis, Verw.-Bezirk)

Religion evang. Stand, Beruf Bildberichterstatter

Personalbeschreibung:

Größe 1.70 m Gestalt untersetzt

Gesicht oval Haar aschblond

Bart — Augen grün-grau

Besondere Kennzeichen (z.B. Brillenträger):

Schuhzeuglänge Schuhzeugweite

(Vor- und Zuname, eigenhändige Unterschrift des Inhabers)

Die Richtigkeit der nicht umrandeten Angaben auf Seiten 1 und 2 und der eigenhändigen Unterschrift des Inhabers bescheinigt

den 16. Oktober 1944

Kommando Nowotny
(Ausfertigender Truppenteil, Dienststelle)

Dienststempel

Major und Kommandeur
(Eigenhändige Unterschrift, Dienstgrad u. Dienststellung des Vorgesetzten)

2

Auszeichnungen!

am	für (Zeit)	Erläuterungen	RM.	Rpf.
Flzgführ.-Abzeichen gem. Verleihungsurkunde Nr. 76179/41 vom 6.5.41				
6.8.42	Ostmedaille 1941/42			
16.9.42	EK 2. Kl.			
14.11.42	Frontflugspange f. Jäger in Gold			
22.11.42	Finnische Freiheitsmedaille 2. Kl.			
22.6.43	EK 1. Kl.			
18.10.43	Ehrenpokal			
21.10.43	Deutsch. Kreuz in Gold			
13.11.43	Verwundetenabzeichen in Schwarz			

Major und Kommandeur

22

The first mission of the *Kommando* takes place on October 7, 1944. The *Rotte* Arnold/Kobert, that took off in Achmer, is surprised and shot down by a "Mustang" of the 361st Fighter Group. While *Leutnant* Arnod saves himself with a parachute, *Leutnant* Kobert fatally crashes. The successful "Mustang" is flown by 1st Lt. Urban L. Drew. The picture above shows Kemp from the 375th Fighter Wing. This picture was taken on October 8, 1944, in Little Walden/Essex. The *Rotte* Schall/Lennartz that took off in Hesepe remains undisturbed, and approaches a *Bomberverband*. *Leutnant* Schall and *Feldwebel* Lennartz each shoot down a B-24 bomber.

Leutnant Franz Schall, head of the *Staffel* in Hesepe, is especially successful in his short time with "*Kommando* Nowotny." Schall, who earlier was on the Eastern Front in JG 52 and known for his series of air victories, is awarded with the *Ritterkreuz* after 117 air victories on October 10, 1944. After the dissolution of "*Kommando* Nowotny" Schall leads *10. Staffel* in the newly formed JG 7. He defeats 14 opponents with the Me 262 until he dies from an explosion of his "Turbo" on April 10, 1945, during a forced landing in Parchim.

Feldwebel Lennartz, an experienced and successful pilot in Lechfeld, proves himself in "*Kommando* Nowotny" with the Me 262.

The strength of the *Kommando* is comprised of 30 Me 262 planes. Many planes crash during forced and outside landings. Engine failure and swarms of birds cause further losses of man and material.

An interesting shot of "Weifle 10" shortly before takeoff. The light, yellow turbine rings are easily recognized.

Haus Wulfhagen in Pente bei Bramsche. Major Walter Nowotny lives here with his staff The house is situated in a very beautiful park, and can hardly be seen from the street today.

After visiting both airports and their facilities, an opportunity arose during the evening to discuss the problems of the unit in detail. Major Nowotny's main concern still was to secure the takeoff and landing of the "Turbos" by propeller-driven planes. The *Platzschutzstaffel*—equipped with Focke-Wulf 190Ds—did their best, but the number of available planes still did not suffice. Disgruntlement arose as *Generaloberst* put the pilots' *Einsatzfreudigkeit* (love of combat) into question.

In the morning Nowotny arrives in the accompaniment of *Generaloberst* Keller in order to inform himself on the development of the *Kommando*.

During the early morning of 8 November both generals met with Major Nowotny for their last conference at the combat post. Strong *Bomberverbände* were reported. The generals remained to observe a *Kommando* mission. Nowotny started the "Dora 9" *Staffeln* (Fw 190D-9). Shortly thereafter the *Rotte* Schall in Hesepe and the *Rotte* Wegmann in Achmer took off. Each *Rotte* reported shootdowns after the first contact with the enemy. *Leutnant* Schall reported that his *Rotte* comrade, *Feldwebel* Daudach, was shot down. Then a new announcement came from Schall: "My plane is on fire! bale out!" Anger and despair came over Nowotny. Maybe he thought about Keller's comment from the previous evening. He called his driver and told Schnörrer: "Come with me, 'Quax,' I'm taking off!" Galland's cry, "Stay here, Nowotny!" remained unheard.

In Achmer "Weifle 8" was ready for takeoff. Nowotny's "Weifle 1" was in the hangar for reconditioning! A pilot in Hesepe received the order to take off, as well, and to meet Nowotny in the air. Nowotny's mission, that seemed to be bad luck from the start, was carried out alone, because the second Me 262 could not start due to a turbine fire. The following sequence of events was only partially covered. Major Nowotny attacked a *Bomberverband* and shot down a "Liberator." That was his 258th air victory. Nowotny removed himself from the *Pulk*. Suddenly he called out nervously into the radio: "Shit, shit—my engine, my engine!"

Was his Me 262 hit during his approach? The statements of those who saw the mission from the combat post are inconsistent. One saw a Me 262 with a burning turbine dive out of a hole in the clouds, falling steeper and steeper until groups of trees and forests above the horizon obstructed the view. The whistling roar ended with a dull explosion. The victor of 258 air victories found his death on this mission. Major Walter Nowotny was no more. Witnesses in Epe, a small place in proximity of the crash site, reported to the author in 1980 that the falling plane suddenly burst in the air, and came down to earth in a burning mass.

Karl Schnörrer drove with his comrades at once to the crash site. They found the parachute halfway opened, hanging on a tree. This seemed to be certain proof that the Me 262 exploded in the air, and that Nowotny tried to bale out at the last minute. The small group rescued what could be salvaged. They wrapped the mortal remains of the dead pilot in the parachute and laid them in a coffin.

The news of Major Nowotny's sudden death spread like wildfire. Shock was everywhere. Who did not sympathize with the family and friends? Who did not see the beaming, boyish laughing of the young pilot in front of them? The name Walter Nowotny has gone down in military aviation history. Walter Nowotny became the epitome of sacrifice and virtue for many of our generation.

Farewell to Walter Nowotny

The *Wehrmachtbericht*, broadcasting companies, and the press report on the death of Major Walter Nowotny. The *Luftwaffe* had once again lost one of their best, as one would say.

See translation p 168

Brillantenträger Major Nowotny gefallen

DAZ Berlin, 9. 11.

Wie der Wehrmachtbericht meldet, hat Gruppenkommandeur Major Walter Nowotny, Inhaber der höchsten deutschen Tapferkeitsauszeichnung, nach Abschuß seines Gegners im Luftkampf den Heldentod gefunden. Mit Major Nowotny, der insgesamt 258 Luftsiege errungen hat, verliert die deutsche Luftwaffe einen ihrer erfolgreichsten Jagdflieger.

Wenn einmal die Geschichte des Ostkrieges geschrieben wird, dann wird der Name des Majors Walter Nowotny, der aus Gmünd im Gau Niederdonau stammt und am 1. Dezember 24 Jahre alt geworden wäre, mit an erster Stelle stehen. Denn Nowotny ist nicht nur für die Luftwaffe, sondern auch für die Soldaten des Heeres ein Begriff gewesen. In vielen hundert Luftkämpfen hat dieser junge und erfolgreiche Jagdflieger, der mit zu den siegreichsten Jagdfliegern der Ostfront gehörte, seinen heldenhaften Einsatz bewiesen.

Er war Jagdflieger im besten Sinne, zäh und „listig", wie es bei den Jägern heißt. Er war hart gegen sich, ging mit einem unheimlichen Angriffsgeist an den Feind und ließ nichts ungenutzt, um seine Taktik und seine Angriffsweise zu vervollkommnen. Den Kampffliegern, die er begleitete, war er bester Schutz und Kamerad und seiner Gruppe, die für ihn durchs Feuer ging, mitreißendes Vorbild und Kamerad zugleich.

Walter Nowotny kam vier Wochen nach Kriegsausbruch zur Luftwaffe. Seit dem Frühjahr 1941 gehörte er zu einem der bekanntesten deutschen Jagdgeschwader, in dem er selbst zu den erfolgreichsten Fliegern und Kämpfern gehörte. Dank seiner Härte, seiner Zähigkeit und seinem unübertrefflichen Angriffswillen hatte er sich sehr schnell in die vorderste Reihe der deutschen Jagdflieger hinaufgekämpft und stand eine geraume Zeit an der Spitze aller deutschen Jagdflieger.

Seine ersten drei Luftsiege erzielte er im Juli 1941 über der Insel Oesel an einem Tage. Nach dem dritten Luftsieg wurde er damals über der Ostsee abgeschossen und erreichte nur unter unsäglichen Anstrengungen in einem Schlauchboot die rettende Küste. Später erzielte Nowotny zweimal je zehn Abschüsse an einem einzigen Tage, und zwei weitere Male schoß er innerhalb von fünf bis zehn Minuten je vier Flugzeuge ab. Als achter Soldat der deutschen Wehrmacht wurde er am 20. Oktober vorigen Jahres mit dem Eichenlaub mit Schwertern und Brillanten zum Ritterkreuz ausgezeichnet.

The coffin of the deceased Major will be laid out in a small chapel, and then led from Epe to Bramsche with military honors. A truck brings his coffin to the railway station, and from then via the train to Vienna. Walter Nowotny finds his last place of rest in his Austrian homeland.

A few days later the *Kommando* is dissolved and transferred back to Lechfeld. After five weeks of missions there are only four Me 262s remaining from the original 30 planes. The *Platzschutz-Staffeln* also suffered great losses. Many of their brave pilots found their last place of rest in Achmer. Until the moment of dissolution successes and losses of "*Kommando* Nowotny" are in a ratio of 1:1. Despite this, the Me 262 has best proven itself as a fighter plane. *Oberst* Steinhoff is assigned to the deployment of a *Turbinenjäger-Geschwader*. The core of the *Geschwader* (JG 7) is the pilots of "*Kommando* Nowotny" and the *Erprobungskommando* Lechfeld.

At the crash site in Epe comrades erect a monument for their young *Kommandeur.* The white marble commemorative plaque should always remind one that Walter Nowotny gave his young life here.

E-Kommando Nowotny

Werk No.			
170044	10/4/44	Hespe crashed during turn in to landing 75% Single-engine landing	Oblt. Teumer
170292	10/5/44	Braunschweig forced highway landing due to fuel shortage 10%	Ofw. Baudach
110405	10/7/44	Achmer shot down at takeoff	Lt. Kobert
110395	10/7/44	Achmer burst after bombardment	Ofhr. Russel
170307	10/7/44	Achmer shot down at takeoff	Oblt. Arnold
110402	10/12/44	Bramel forced landing fuel shortage 10%	Fw. Lennartz
110339	10/13/44	Achmer crashed at takeoff 99% Takeoff with following wind across country, tip of fuselage pulled too soon	Obering. Leithner
110401	10/13/44	Hesepe runway damage during landing	Ofhr. Russel
170041	10/4/44	Braunschweig Waggum shock strut broke out at landing 25%	Lt. Schall
110388	10/12/44	Steenwyk forced landing due to fuel shortage 15%	Oblt. Bley
110387	10/29/44	Nordhorn rammed during air combat 99%	Lt. Schreiber
110481	10/28/44	Achmer crashed at takeoff 99%	Oblt. Bley
110419	10/28/44	Hesepe nose wheel not lowered during landing	Lt. Schall
110386	11/1/44	Holland shot down 99%	Ofhr. Banzhaff
110368	11/2/44	Achmer single-motor flight crash 99% recovered alive	Uffz. Zöllner
170278	11/2/44	Achmer runway damage 30%	Ofw. Göbel
170210	11/4/44	Single-motor landing 95%	Ofw. Zander
110403	11/4/44	Bohmte forced landing 95%	Ofw. Göbel
110483	11/4/44	Lüneburg supposedly shot down 99%	Ofhr. Banzhaff
110389	11/6/44	?50%	Lt. Spangenberg
170045	11/6/44	Hespe shock strut broke out at landing	Ofw. Büttner
110402	11/6/44	Ahlhorn forced landing fuel shortage 30%	Ofw. Freutzer
110490	11/6/44	by Bremen forced landing fuel shortage 30%	Ofw. Lennartz
110400	11/8/44	Crash after enemy attack 100%	Major Nowotny
110404	11/8/44	At 900 m engine stalled after enemy efforts 100% parachute jump	Lt. Schall
170293	11/8/44	Tires burst at takeoff	Fw. Büttner

On November 8, 1944, supplies on four planes melted down. Two days later transferred to Lechfeld for replenishment.
The *Kommando* had a total of 30 planes, 26 of which broke down.
The *Kommando* achieved 22 shootdowns, from which 4 are probable.

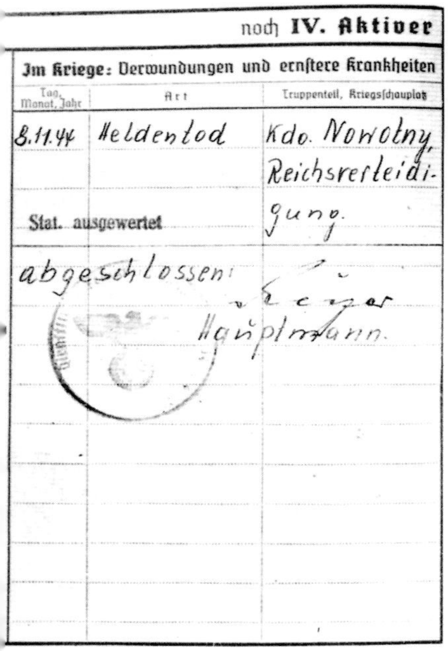

noch **IV. Aktiver**

Im Kriege: Verwundungen und ernstere Krankheiten

Tag, Monat, Jahr	Art	Truppenteil, Kriegsschauplatz
8.11.44	Heldentod	Kdo. Nowotny Reichsverteidigung
Stat. ausgewertet		

abgeschlossen: Kreger(?) Hauptmann.

Last entry into Walter Nowotny's service record book.

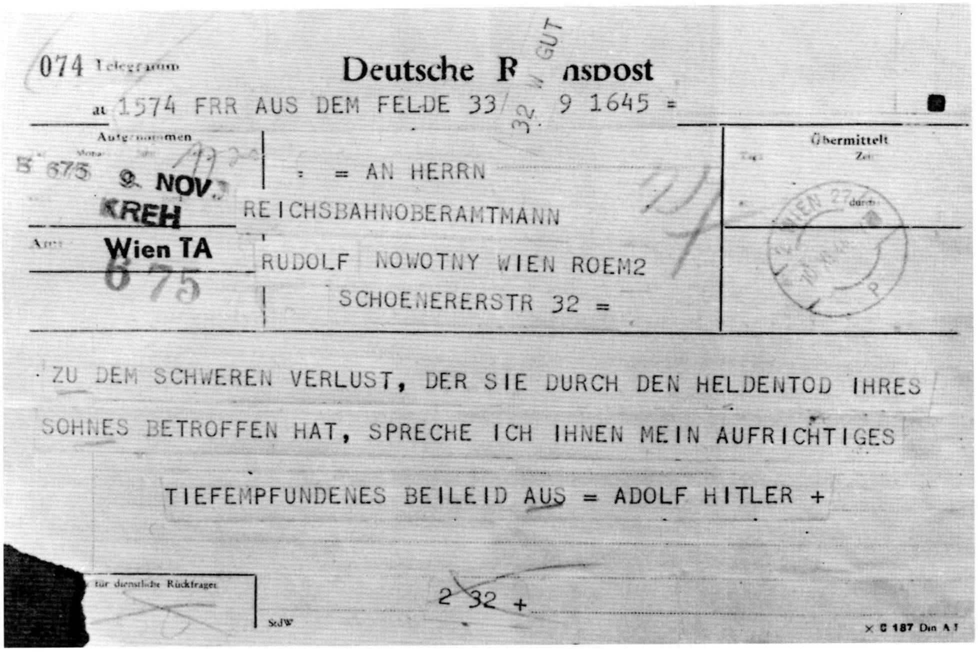

074 Telegramm Deutsche R[eich]spost

at 1574 FRR AUS DEM FELDE 33/32 9 1645 =

Aufgenommen: 9. NOV. KREH Wien TA 675

= AN HERRN
REICHSBAHNOBERAMTMANN
RUDOLF NOWOTNY WIEN ROEM2
SCHOENERERSTR 32 =

Übermittelt

ZU DEM SCHWEREN VERLUST, DER SIE DURCH DEN HELDENTOD IHRES SOHNES BETROFFEN HAT, SPRECHE ICH IHNEN MEIN AUFRICHTIGES TIEFEMPFUNDENES BEILEID AUS = ADOLF HITLER +

für dienstliche Rückfragen

2 32 +

Hitler's sympathy telegram to the parents in Vienna.

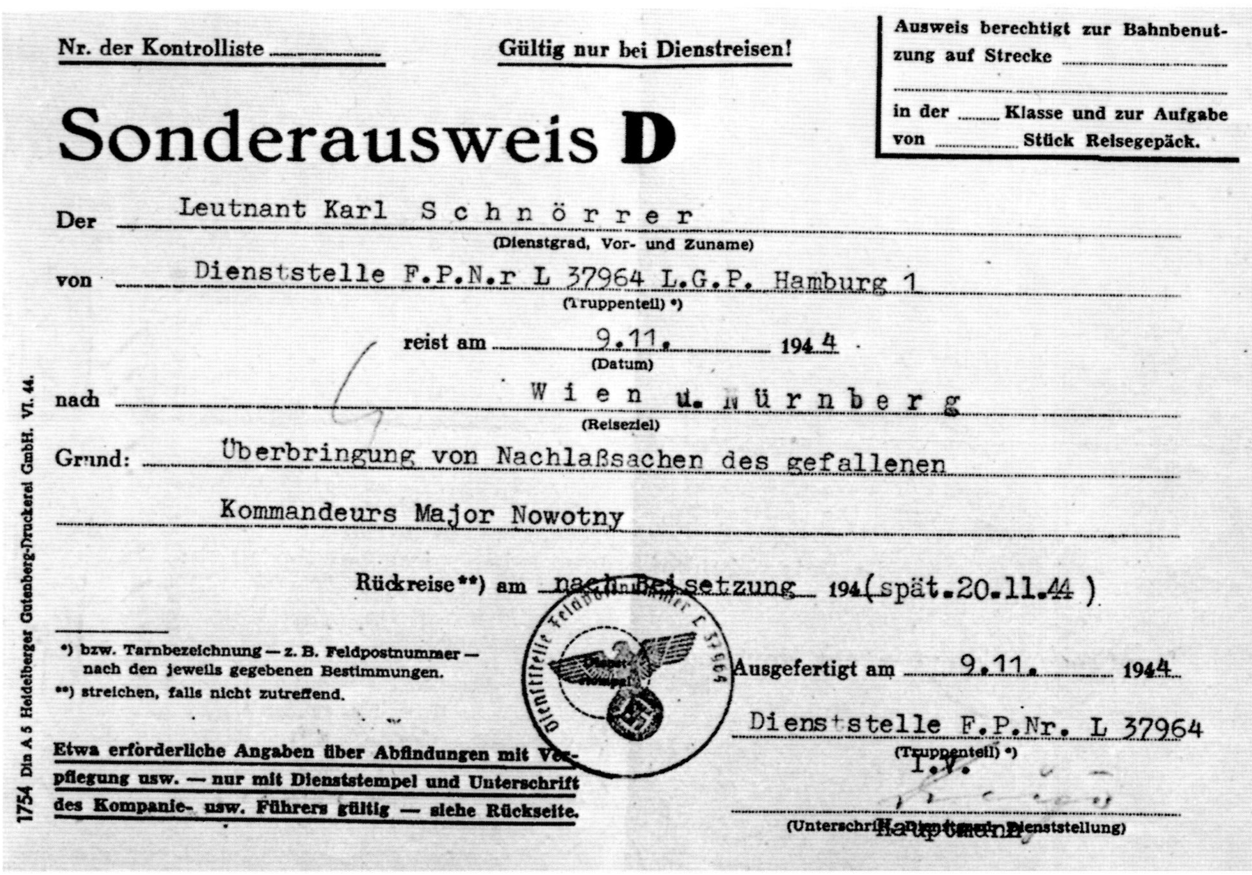

Nr. der Kontrolliste ....

Gültig nur bei Dienstreisen!

Ausweis berechtigt zur Bahnbenutzung auf Strecke .... in der ...... Klasse und zur Aufgabe von ...... Stück Reisegepäck.

Sonderausweis D

Der Leutnant Karl S c h n ö r r e r
(Dienstgrad, Vor- und Zuname)

von Dienststelle F.P.N.r L 37964 L.G.P. Hamburg 1
(Truppenteil) *)

reist am 9.11. 1944
(Datum)

nach W i e n u. N ü r n b e r g
(Reiseziel)

Grund: Überbringung von Nachlaßsachen des gefallenen Kommandeurs Major Nowotny

Rückreise**) am ~~nach Beisetzung~~ 194 (spät.20.11.44)

*) bzw. Tarnbezeichnung — z. B. Feldpostnummer — nach den jeweils gegebenen Bestimmungen.
**) streichen, falls nicht zutreffend.

Etwa erforderliche Angaben über Abfindungen mit Verpflegung usw. — nur mit Dienststempel und Unterschrift des Kompanie- usw. Führers gültig — siehe Rückseite.

Ausgefertigt am 9.11. 1944

Dienststelle F.P.Nr. L 37964
(Truppenteil) *)

I.V.

(Unterschrift, Dienstgrad, Dienststellung) Hauptmann

1754 Din A 5 Heidelberger Gutenberg-Druckerei GmbH. VI. 44.

ID card for Leutnant Karl Schnörrer.

November 15, 1944: State ceremony in the ceremonial hall of the Wiener Hofburg.

The coffin, covered with imperial war flags, and topped with Walter Nowotny's cap and officer's sword. His loyal friend, "Quax" Schnörrer, carries the decoration pillow, then *Oberst* Gollob. Four highly decorated officers of the *Luftwaffe* are on sentry duty. (Front from left: Major Strüning, Major Schönert, in the back: Major Fözö and Major Christl.) For the *General der Jagdflieger*, Galland, who was unable to come, *Generaloberst* Deflloch holds the funeral oration, and lays a wreath down on behalf of Hitler

Generaloberst Deflloch expresses condolences to the members of the family. From the left: Rudolf Nowotny, the oldest brother of Walter Nowotny, Walter's bride, the father, *Generaloberst* Deflloch, and the mother half hidden.

After the state ceremony Nowotny's coffin is brought to the *Zentralfriedhof* on a carriage. The Viennese people say goodbye to their great pilot, whom they celebrated only a year before.

The funeral procession into the *Zentralfriedhof* is led by *Oberleutnant* Franz Schall The sky is somber above Vienna, and the torches of the *Hitlerjungen* try in vain to lighten the dismal mood of those present.

"Live well, my good comrade!" With these words Nowotny's former *Kommodore*, *Oberst* Trautlof, ended his commemorative address at his grave. *Oberst* Trautloft remembers Nowotny's great deeds on the Eastern Front, and his comradeship that made such achievements possible. He also remembers the conversation in the circle of those in JG 54, as the discussion came to a soldier's death. "Nowi" said then, "I don't want to die an old man, but depart at the height of the celebration!"

In Remembrance

On June 22, 1958, during a ceremony at the honored grave in Vienna's *Zentralfriedhof*, the unveiling of a memorial takes place. By fundraising in all of upper Austria, the financing of the memorial was made possible. Approximately 1200 people take part in the unveiling, from Germany the chairmen of the *Gemeinschaft der Jagdflieger* e. V., Werner Andres, and Theo Osterkamp for the *Gemeinschaft der Ritterkreuzträger*, lay down a wreath. The bearer of Germany's highest medal for bravery, *Oberst* Hans-Ulrich Rudel, comes from South America to Vienna to pay respect to his dead comrade.

The first tombstone that commemorates the young pilot in Vienna's *Zentralfriedhof*. After the war, cows graze on Austria's honored graves. Walter Nowotny finds his last place of rest in an honored grave in Vienna, surrounded by graves of the worthiest sons of Austria.

Every year on *Totensonntag* the inhabitants remember their unforgettable Walter Nowotny. In the picture: ceremonial laying of the wreath by Dr. Josef Lenz and Josef Fözö from the Austrian *Aeroclub*.

Generalleutnant A. D. Galland, Walter Nowotny's former *Waffengeneral*, speaks a few words of remembrance at his 50th birthday, and lays down a bouquet of flowers.

A document of a very rare kind is portrayed in this sculpture in a clay-state, red tone. A talented soldier, who served in "*Kommando* Nowotny," probably modeled his *Kommandeur* after a picture. On the wooden base it states that Nowotny died from an explosion of the "Turbo." The sculpture was damaged during an attack on *Platz Achmer*. It should now be undergoing restoration and be finding a worthy home.

In 1981 the *Institut für Münz- und Medaillenkunst*, Munich and Vienna, made coins commemorating the former pilot. The black and white picture of the Nowotny coin shows their excellent work.

Walter Nowotny's grave in Vienna. The fresh flowers and the pristine condition are proof that Walter Nowotny will remain unforgotten in the hearts of men.

Abbreviations

Adj	Adjutant
EK	Eisernes Kreuz
EL	Eichenlaub
Erpr.Kdo	Erprobungskommando
	(original meaning: Funkentelegraphie: in the Luftwaffe a term for Funk-/Funksprech-)
Fw.	Feldwebel
Hptm	Hauptmann
JG	Jagdgeschwader
KG	Kampfgeschwader
Lt.	Leutnant (1st Lt. - US-Oberleutnant)
MG	Maschinengewehr
N.Ö.	Niederösterreich
Oberstlt.	Oberstleutnant
Oblt.	Oberleutnant
Ofw.	Oberfeldwebel
Prof.	Professor
Schw.	Schwerter
St.G.	Stukageschwader
Uffz.	Unteroffizier
ZG	Zerstörergeschwader

Staffeln/Kompanien and *Geschwader/Regimenter* are numbered with Arabic numerals, *Gruppen* with Roman numerals.

A Word of Thanks

With ceaseless effort and great care this book came about; it only took shape with the selfless help of many friends.

Special thanks goes to Herr Dipl.-Kaufmann Rudolf Nowotny from Linz/Donau and his family. Because of their help it was possible to clearly portray Nowotny, the man, to the reader of the book. Pictures, documents, and letters from the family's archive form the core of this illustrated book. I must also thank the following people for their support:

Manfred Boehme, Mörfelden
Georg Christl, Ransbach-Baumbach
Urban L. Drew, Pretoria/Südafrika
Georg-Peter Eder, Wiesbaden
Karl Fischer, Konstanz
Adolf Galland, Oberwinter
Hans Höhler, Essen
Wolfgang Kretschmer, Haan
Adolf Lanzenbacher, Wien/Österreich
Erich Nickolai, Saarbrücken
Ernst Obermaier, München
Ernst Richter, Wardenburg
Karl Schnörrer, Nürnberg
Roswitha Schnörrer, Nürnberg
Ernst Schröder, Bonn/Röttgen
Rudi Sinner, Linz/Donau
Hannes Trautloft, Baden-Baden

Werner Held

Bibliography

Nowotny, Rudolf: *Walter Nowotny*, Leoni, 1973

Galland, Adolf: *The First and the Last*, Darmstadt, 1953

Obermaier, Ernst: *The Bearers of the Ritterkreuz of the Luftwaffe*, Mainz, 1966

Priller, Josef: *History of a Jagdgeschwader*, Heidelberg, 1962

Jägerblatt: *Official Organ of the Gemeinschaft der Jagdflieger*

Luftwaffen-Illustrierte: *Der Adler*, all age groups

Obermaier/Ring: *Jagdflieger*

Ziegler, Mano: *Turbinen-Jäger Me 262*, Stuttgart, 1977

Translation of News Article

(see p 152)

Bearer of the *Brillant* Major Nowotny Has Fallen / DAZ Berlin 11/9

As the *Wehrmachtbericht* reported, *Gruppenkommandeur* Major Walter Nowotny, bearer of the highest German medal for bravery, has found a hero's death after a shootdown of his opponent in air combat. With Major Nowotny, who won a total of 258 air victories, the German *Luftwaffe* loses one of their most successful fighter pilots.

When the history of the eastern war is written, the name Major Walter Nowotny, who is from Gmünd, in Gau Niederdonau, and would have been 24 years old on 1 December, will come first. Nowotny is a household name, not only for the *Luftwaffe*, but also for the soldiers of the army. In many hundreds of air combat missions this young and successful fighter pilot, who is considered one of the most victorious fighter pilots on the Eastern Front, has proved his heroic dedication.

He was a fighter pilot in the best sense, tough and "cunning," as the *Jäger* say. He was hard on himself, had a fantastic *Angriffsgeist* against the enemy, and stopped at nothing to perfect his tactics and methods of attack. To the *Kampfflieger* that he accompanied he was the best protection and comrade and, to his *Gruppe*, who went through hell with him, an exciting role model and comrade at the same time.

Four weeks after the war broke out Walter Nowotny came to the *Luftwaffe*. Since the spring of 1941 he belonged to the most famous German *Jagdgeschwader*, in which he himself was one of the most successful pilots and fighters. Thanks to his toughness and his unsurpassable *Angriffswillen* he struggled his way to the first row of German fighter pilots, and stood for a fairly long time at the top of all the German fighter pilots.

He won his first three air victories in July 1941 above the island Ösel in one day. After the third air victory he was shot down above the Baltic sea, and reached the coast in a life raft by unspeakable efforts. Nowotny later twice achieved ten shootdowns in a single day, and twice within five to ten minutes he shot down four planes. As the eighth soldier of the German *Wehrmacht* he was awarded with the *Eichenlaub mit Schwerten und Brillanten zum Ritterkreuz* on 20 October.

He found a hero's death after he won 258 air victories. His comrades, in whom his spirit will live on, and the German people will never forget his name and his deeds.